Advance praise for *Saint Clare: Beyond the Legend*

"Marco Bartoli's book is not a biography but a dialogue between silence and memory, between what has been said and what has not been said about Clare of Assisi, between evidence and interpretation. Entering into dialogue with the most important source for knowing Clare, *The Legend of Saint Clare the Virgin*, Bartoli offers an insightful, critical study of the woman who was called the 'strongest stone of the whole foundation.' Those who are familiar with Clarian studies will find this work a welcome contribution to the ongoing reconstruction of the woman of Assisi. For the unfamiliar reader, Bartoli provides a fascinating and lucid account of one of the most remarkable women of the Middle Ages." —Ilia Delio, O.S.F., author, *Franciscan Prayer* and *Clare of Assisi: A Heart Full of Love*

"By drawing on a variety of sources—historical, biographical, spiritual, Franciscan—Marco Bartoli challenges us to seriously review our preconceived ideas of Clare. She may indeed have been the 'little plant' of Francis of Assisi, but this book eloquently demonstrates that Clare grew into her own 'tree': strong, enduring, deeply, and firmly rooted in her own understanding and living of the gospel. Clare comes through not just as 'Saint' Clare but as Clare the person, and what an inspiring, challenging, and attractive person she is." —Brother Séamus Mulholland, O.F.M., Franciscan International Study Centre

"The research and the publications of the past decades have definitively demonstrated that Clare was not Francis' silent shadow, nor was she a nun buried in the enclosure of a monastery. Continuing to cast light on the real Clare through this book, Marco Bartoli describes her as she was known and acknowledged in her time: as a woman of great reputation, courtesy, and beauty. He also restores the true relationship of Clare and Francis, the poor sister and the lesser brother, so close to one another in their evangelical life and yet so different in their personalities. With Marco Bartoli's book, the true Clare emerges." —Jean François Godet-Calogeras, The Franciscan Institute, St. Bonaventure University

"Marco Bartoli's *Clare of Assisi: Beyond the Legend* leaves no stone unturned in his search for the truth about Clare that lies beneath the legend. He works like an archeologist sifting through shards of literary evidence to unearth an accurate portrait of Clare of Assisi that reaches beyond her legend. His tools are a mind schooled in the historical method and his extensive knowledge of medieval literature, society, and culture. Mix this with his expertise and reputation as a Franciscan historian, and what results is a fresh and fascinating picture of Clare in the midst of the key players in her life. Bartoli's latest book on Clare may well come to be recognized in our time as the definitive biography of Clare. It is undisputedly the most comprehensive treatment to date of the primary sources underlying the popular understanding of Clare's story." —Ingrid Peterson, O.S.F., author, *Clare of Assisi: A Biographical Study*

"*Clare: Beyond the Legend* opens with a tantalizing question: Did Clare of Assisi ever exist? This perplexing question arises from that fact that Clare Offreduccio is never mentioned in Francis' writings nor does Thomas of Celano refer to her in the Second Life. Clare might have remained a silent unknown woman of the Middle Ages had the 800th anniversary of her birth not spurred research into the mystery of her existence. Bartoli gleans vital information from multiple conferences held during the 800th anniversary celebrations to create a new spiritual-historical portrait of the noblewoman of Assisi who chose a life of poverty. From the silence of her monastery life, Clare became the custodian of Franciscan memory. Bartoli brings Clare from silence to modern memory with interest and integrity." —Patricia Normile, S.F.O., author, *John Dear on Peace: An Introduction to His Life and Work*

53 – decisive moment for Clare
58 – status of Clare at her "Tonsure"

SAINT CLARE

SAINT
CLARE
beyond the legend

MARCO BARTOLI
TRANSLATED BY SISTER FRANCES TERESA DOWNING, O.S.C.

Franciscan
International Study Centre

ST. ANTHONY MESSENGER PRESS
Cincinnati, Ohio

Cover and book design by Mark Sullivan

Cover art, "St. Clare of Assisi," by Glenn Lowcock. Used with permission of the artist.

LIBRARY OF CONGRESS CATALOGING-IN-PUBLICATION DATA
Bartoli, Marco.
[Chiara. English]
Saint Clare : beyond the legend / Marco Bartoli ; translated by Frances Teresa Downing.
p. cm.
Includes bibliographical references.
ISBN 978-0-86716-950-8 (pbk. : alk. paper) 1. Clare, of Assisi, Saint, 1194–1253. I.
Downing, Frances Teresa. II. Title.
BX4700.C6B3813 2010
271'.97302—dc22
[B]
2009053220

ISBN 978-0-86716-950-8
FISC ISBN 978-0-9549272-5-7

Translated from the Italian edition, Chiara: Una donna tra silenzio e memoria, published by
Edizioni San Paolo, S.R.L., ©2001, 2003.

Published by St. Anthony Messenger Press
28 W. Liberty St.
Cincinnati, OH 45202
www.SAMPBooks.org

Printed in the United States of America.

Printed on acid-free paper.

10 11 12 13 14   5 4 3 2 1

TRANSLATOR'S NOTES

Marco Bartoli's style is deceptively simple. It is this which has made him such a good teacher over the years, and I have done my best to retain that clarity and simplicity of style in the translation.

With regard to footnotes—the references in the Italian text are extensive and numerous. However there seemed little point in adding references to works only available in Italian, so I have had to make some decisions about what to retain and what to remove. In the end, I decided to be consistent with Marco Bartoli's earlier volume, *Clare of Assisi,* and simply keep the following:

- references to the sources, and to give the text reference not the page number in the various collections of sources. However, Clare's Letters, Rule, Testament and Blessing, the Canonisation Process, the Legend and various other relevant documents can all be found in *Clare of Assisi: Early Documents, The Lady.* This is the 2006 revised edition;
- for quotations from Clare's writings, I have given the letter reference and its verse, e.g., 2Ag13, and not the page reference in *Clare of Assisi: Early Documents;*
- for quotations from Francis' writings, I have followed the same principle and given the reference to the actual writing, not to the page in the *Omnibus of Sources,* although all the texts are in those volumes should anyone wish to pursue matters.

- references to the Bullarium Franciscanum, since this is also a source document and available in Franciscan libraries;
- references to the Archivum Franciscanum Historicum and the Analecta Franciscana, for the same reasons.
- references which struck me as particularly interesting.
- for Scripture I have used the *Living Bible* version.

There are a few exceptions to the above, mainly when Bartoli has quoted another author and then the footnote simply gives the reference although (probably) in Italian. I have omitted references to Migne's *Patrologia Series Graeca* and *Series Latina*. Those who want or need these can probably find them for themselves or are able to check in the Italian edition. Such pruning inevitably means that interesting snippets of information are lost to the English reader, but this seemed preferable to multiplying references to inaccessible information. I hope readers who disagree will forgive me for what might seem arbitrary. For consistency, I have used the translation of Clare's writings from *The Lady* unless these seem in conflict with the text used by Bartoli in such a way that the point of the quotation would be lost. In that situation, I have made my own translation.

This work has been far too long in the doing and I would like to thank all those who have supported, encouraged and endured me during that time. I am especially grateful to Sister Pat of the Poor Clares, Arundel, for her careful proofreading and for checking all the footnotes, a tedious and time-consuming work, which she did with speed and wonderful accuracy.

Hollington,
4 October 2008

AF	Analecta Franciscana
AFH	Archivum Franciscanum Historicum
BF	Bullarium Franciscanum
1 Cel★★	Thomas of Celano, *First Life of Saint Francis*
2 Cel★★	Thomas of Celano, *Remembrance of the desires of a soul*
FF★★	*Fontes Francescane,* 2 Vols, Assisi 1977
LegCl.★	*Legend of St Clare the Virgin*
LegPer★	*Legend of Perugia* or *The Assisi Compilation*
PG	*Patrologia cursus completus. Series graeca* ed. J.-P. Migne, 217 vol., Paris 1844–1855
CanProc.★	*Canonisation Process of St Clare*
RegCl.★¹	*Rule of St Clare*
RnB	*Regula non bullata*
LegMaj	*Legenda Maior of Bonaventure*
ConstHug	*Constitutions of Hugolino*

CONTENTS

FOREWORD

Saint Clare: Beyond the Legend is, in one sense, a how-to-read book. How do you read the first "life" of Saint Clare, the so-called *Legend of Saint Clare the Virgin*?

Marco Bartoli's helpful insight is that the best way to read the *Legend of Saint Clare the Virgin* is to read it in conjunction with and illumined by another text that precedes it, *The Acts of the Process of Canonization of Saint Clare*. This latter text, because it consists of the testimony of eye witnesses, including Clare's own sisters, who attest to the life and sanctity of Clare before and after her life as a Franciscan, is the most reliable of the texts we have, with the exception of Saint Clare's own writings.

This book, then, is a reexamination of who Clare of Assisi was as far as we can know from the Process of Canonization and the Legend. Better than any text I've read to date, this book provides the reader with an accurate, balanced picture of Clare as the first Franciscan woman, especially if read in conjunction with its companion volume, *Clare of Assisi*. The latter is Bartoli's biography of Saint Clare, while *Saint Clare: Beyond the Legend* is a comparative study of two of the earliest sources of Saint Clare's life and of the lives and spirituality of Clare and her sisters at San Damiano.

In using the Process of Canonization to help fill in and illumine the Legend of Saint Clare, Bartoli explores all of the significant problematic and rich terms in both texts in order to better understand who Clare really was.

Such a task requires the mind and knowledge of an experienced medieval scholar such as Bartoli. And this book, like his previous book, *Clare of Assisi*, have been translated by the English Poor Clare, Sister Frances Teresa Downing, which further enriches the present English translation. Sister Frances Teresa, herself an author and scholar of Saint Clare, brings to the text the further advantage of one who has lived the Rule of Saint Clare, as well as the skill and insight of a practiced translator.

Bartoli and Downing offer the English reader a rich and fascinating tapestry of historical fact, philology, and close reading of the text that "connects the dots" in a significant area of Clare studies. All of which may sound off-putting to some readers, but there is also about this book the feel of a text that should be read meditatively, a kind of *lectio divina*, in that the care and reverence with which Bartoli approaches his subject leads the reader into the life of a woman who was and is the saint one prays to and tries to emulate. The very title, *Beyond the Legend*, invites a reading that is more than what may be perceived as something to be read only by scholars.

Though scholarly in method, the language of the present volume is simple and unadorned and illumines aspects of the Middle Ages that relate importantly to Saint Clare, such as the tradition of courtly love and the meaning of medieval tonsure, to mention two. Such explorations help the reader understand some of the terms Saint Clare uses and also the breadth and depth of her knowledge of the ethos of medieval Umbria, the medieval church, and of the possibilities for women, both in society and in the church.

The examination of Saint Clare's relationship to the papacy contextualizes brilliantly the ongoing drama of Clare's determination to have her and her sisters' Rule of Life approved by the pope—a dream that is finally realized on her deathbed.

Each of the chapters is written clearly and without fuss so that one comes away confident that the content is the condensation of years of research and thought. Marco Bartoli is not only a scholar; he is a clear and persuasive writer. If one would know Saint Clare of Assisi, it would be hard to find a more reliable guide.

Murray Bodo, O.F.M.

Assisi, Italy

September 26, 2009

INTRODUCTION

There are a number of reasons why Clare of Assisi can be defined as a woman between silence and memory. The first reason is because of her own personal story. Clare in fact, chose to live her whole life hidden in a monastic silence, so much so that in the *First Life of St Francis*, Thomas of Celano says that she and her sisters

> . . . have so attained the unique grace of abstinence and silence that they scarcely need to exert any effort to check the promptings of the flesh and to restrain their tongues. Some among them are so unused to speaking that when they are constrained by some necessity they have almost forgotten the proper way to pronounce the words.[2]

On the other hand, Clare is the first woman of the Middle Ages to have broken this wall of silence. While the great majority of medieval women in the sources are mute, the voice of Clare speaks through her writings even to the present day.

In the sources, silence and memory are like two extremes of the situation concerning this woman of Assisi. On the one hand, the witnesses speak up and on the other, they are silent. Who was this Clare of Assisi? The more we burrow into the documents of the thirteenth century, the more radical becomes the question: did Clare of Assisi ever exist? This echoes the question of Jacques le Goff in his magisterial biography of Louis IX.[3] It is true that if we only read the writings of Francis, we might well doubt the Assisi woman's existence since Clare is not named even once. Turning the pages of some lovely insights from Jacques Delarun[4], we could legitimately come to think that Clare never 'passed through' Francis' life. The saint never names his first disciple.

Between silence and memory: any attempt to make an historical reconstruction of the profile of the woman of Assisi must inevitably play between these two extremes, not only the silence of Francis, but also the silence of other Franciscan sources—or at least some of them. So, for instance, in his *First Life of Francis*, written by Thomas of Celano between 1228 and 1230, Clare is given such a eulogy as to be almost embarrassing, while in the so-called *Second Life* by the same Thomas of Celano, composed almost fifteen years later, Clare has vanished altogether and her name is not even mentioned. What is the reason for this (certainly censorious) decision?

Silence and memory are also the two characteristics of the 'place' of San Damiano where Clare chose to live in the company of some dozens of companions, for more than forty years of her life. It is certainly a space for silence, given its character of a monastic cloister, but San Damiano has also become the place of memory because Clare, during those long years when she outlived Francis, became a shrewd custodian of the Franciscan memory. According to the evidence of Ubertino of Casale, the *rotuli* or scrolls with the companions' precious memories of Francis were preserved at San Damiano.

Why turn again to speak about Clare, given the fact that the author has already written a biography of her more than ten years ago? At the time when that work was published (1989) there were not many works devoted to the story of the lady, and in particular not many monographs devoted to a single feminine figure, especially of one as widely known as the saint of Assisi. On the other hand, in spite of some extremely relevant historical and Franciscan productions, critical works dedicated to the first disciple of Francis were, at that time, fairly rare. Perhaps because of this lacuna, the earlier work had unexpected good fortune and was translated into various languages. Since then there have appeared dozens of studies and works on Clare and on the religious communities which, under various titles, held on to her experience. In 1993–1994 came the eighth centenary of her birth which gave the chance for meetings and scholarly conventions in every part of the world. Since then, learned contributions have multiplied.

To turn and speak again about Clare does not mean a new biography, with the inevitable risk of repetition, nor an attempt to sum up all the studies on the matter, which would require yet another convention. To turn and speak again of Clare is precisely to enter into this dialogue between silence and memory, between what has been said and what has not been said, between evidence and interpretation. In other words, it means to enter into dialogue with the most important source for knowing Clare of Assisi, the *Legenda sanctae Clarae virginis, The Legend of Saint Clare the Virgin*, written by order of the pope on the occasion of her canonisation. Here we are analysing not the 'true' Clare (as if according to some scientific reconstruction of the truth with unarguable conclusions) but, more modestly, trying to seek out the memory of Clare as she has been interpreted, filtered and transmitted through this biography.

Like many things, this present work had a chance beginning. Some while back, it fell to me to prepare a new Italian translation of the *Legend*. Actually taking the text in hand reminded me of the guidelines which Raoul Manselli had given me when I was a young student. He invited me to read a hagiographic text 'in the light of', which means here to read the *Legend* in the light of the Acts of the Canonisation Process which were the direct source for the *Legend*.

While I was working on that translation I saw more clearly that an avenue of study was opening up, that of reading the text of the *Legend* in a modern, and therefore scientific, manner. So this is not a new biography but a new reading of an old biography. In other words, we are not here dealing with 'the Clare of history' so much as 'the Clare of the *Legend*', the presentation of Clare which her biographer made. It is also obvious that the other sources, as well as allowing some judgements of the old biography, can also help us to a further understanding of 'the Clare of history'.

In recent years, studies of Clare of Assisi have moved ahead considerably, given wing by the eighth centenary of her birth, as has been said. On that occasion, congresses and international gatherings multiplied and studies from various starting points abounded, all having an interest in the woman of Assisi, all producing highly interesting contributions. On the other hand, such studies would not have been possible if the centenary had not fallen at a moment when the attention of many was focussed on new fields of research, particularly that of the history of women and their holiness.

At the end of one such historical convention for the centenary, some scholars, among them Alfonso Marini, Maria Pia Alberzoni, Jacques Delarun, expressed their desire to seek some such balance themselves. There was a place for a new synthesis of knowledge about the life and experience of the woman of Assisi. While it is not yet the moment for unanimity, there is still something to be gained from considering the results of recent historical research into Clare. The pages which follow are, in some sense, a relaunching of that dialogue with these friends as well as with others who are interested in Clare, and in this way making sure that the avenues of research opened by the centenary will not be abandoned.

CLARE OF ASSISI — WHO WAS SHE?

Clare of Assisi—who was she? The
first person to answer this question was Thomas of Celano, author of
the *First Life of Francis of Assisi*. In some well known words, he first
evokes the church of San Damiano where Francis lived for a while
at the beginning of his venture, and then adds:

> This is the blessed and holy place where the glorious religion and
> most excellent Order of Poor Ladies and holy virgins had its happy
> beginning, about six years after the conversion of the blessed
> Francis and through that same blessed man. The Lady Clare, a
> native of the city of Assisi, the most precious and strongest stone
> of the whole structure, stands as the foundation for all the other
> stones. For after the beginning of the Order of Brothers, when this
> lady was converted to God through the counsel of the holy man,
> she lived for the good of many and as an example to countless oth-
> ers. Noble by lineage, but more noble by grace, chaste in body,
> most chaste in mind, young in age, mature in spirit, steadfast in
> purpose and most eager in her desire for divine love, endowed

with wisdom and excelling in humility, bright in name, more brilliant in life, most brilliant in character.[5]

Without doubt this is a page of propaganda. The official life of any new saint was destined to be read throughout Christendom. The author must have judged it useful to insert this description of Clare into a text dedicated to Francis, perhaps thinking of an eventual female public. Probably, too, the one who commissioned the *Legend* was of one mind with him, meaning Pope Gregory IX who, before he became pope and when he was simply a cardinal, had delighted in his close friendship with Francis and Clare, and had directly influenced the evolution of the Order. Thomas of Celano then goes a little further. Having drawn an extremely flattering spiritual portrait of the *sisters* who were living at San Damiano, he then explicitly attributes the institution of their way of life to the Pope:

> Their wondrous life and their renowned practices received from the Lord Pope Gregory, at that time bishop of Ostia, would require another book and the leisure in which to write it.[6]

This description of Clare inserted into the *Life of Francis of Assisi*, then, served the function of evoking other feminine vocations to that Order which had been instituted by the Pope himself. The most striking thing, though, is that at the time when the *Legend* was written, that is between 1228 and 1230, Clare was no more than thirty-six years old. Usually, one waits for the death of the person concerned before writing the pages of hagiography! Here Thomas of Celano did not want to wait and, as early as 1230, presented Clare as a saint to be imitated. No other disciple of Francis was accorded such an honour.[7]

So who was this Clare of Assisi and why, even while still alive, was she presented as a saint? What was it about her? As Thomas of Celano says, she was of noble birth. In the thirteenth century, as André Vauchez has shown in his magisterial work on the process of canonisation, nobility was a prerequisite for the canonisation of a woman. Clare's nobility was not of the highest rank, at least when compared with the other saints offered for canonisation in that century who were queens or at least royalty. On the other hand, when we look more closely, we see that the virtues described by Thomas are all rooted in the lack of something. They are presented in this way: Clare, although not of the highest aristocratic rank was, however, noble through grace; although still relatively young—an obvious defect—she was indeed mature in spirit; although animated by enthusiastic love—something which could be really dangerous—she was filled with wisdom and an incomparable humility. Looking closely we see that Thomas has actually only recognised two genuine virtues in Clare: that she was physically a virgin and that she was called Clare. Even these only served to underline the fact that she was a virgin spiritually and that, named Clare, she had above all 'clarity' in her life and virtue.

This hagiographic construction at least makes it clear that this is the portrait of a young girl, from an aristocratic family of modest importance, who left it in order to give herself, enthusiastically, to the path indicated by Francis of Assisi. Thomas says that Clare was *in divino amore ardentissima desiderio*: 'all burning with desire for the love of God'. This enthusiasm had been personally verified a few years earlier by Gregory IX himself while he was in Assisi (probably for the canonisation of Francis in 1228). Gregory, as has been said, had already known Clare for some time, and ever since the time when he was Cardinal Legate in Umbria, had shown himself full of solicitude for the community at San Damiano. On this occasion, he was preoccupied with ensuring that the monastery had a minimal income, or at least that they did not go on living in absolute uncertainty. As the *Legend of St Clare the Virgin* says:

> Pope Gregory of happy memory, a man as very worthy of the papal throne as he was venerable in his deeds, loved this holy woman intensely with a fatherly affection. When he was attempting to persuade her that, because of the events of the times and the dangers of the world, she should consent to have some possessions which he himself willingly offered, she resisted with a very strong spirit and would in no way acquiesce. To this the Pope replied: 'If you fear for your vow, We absolve you from it.' 'Holy Father', she said, 'I will never in any way wish to be absolved from the following of Christ.'[8]

Clare not only refused the pope's suggestion, but even more, maintained that such a suggestion went against the Gospel itself. On a number of other occasions, the young woman had shown this same remarkable liberty of spirit, for instance on the day when she heard of the martyrdom of the first Franciscans sent into Morocco. As Sr Cecilia says in the Canonisation Process:

> The Lady Clare had such a fervent spirit she willingly wanted to endure martyrdom for love of the Lord. She showed this when, after she had heard certain brothers had been martyred in Morocco, she said she wanted to go there. Then, because of this, the witnesses wept. This was before she was so sick.[9]

This kind of behaviour was the complete opposite of that traditionally assigned to a woman, and especially to an abbess responsible for a community of sisters. Clare, following Francis' example, intended to leave everything in order to bear witness to the Gospel.

With all this in mind, Thomas's decision to insert this eulogy of

Clare into the official life of Francis was not without risk. He did so precisely because it was the mind of the one commissioning the work, namely the pope. At the time when he became pope, Gregory IX had been confronted with the problem of the monasteries of 'Poor Ladies, Recluses'[10] whom he had founded in Umbria and Tuscany and who he was directing right up to the moment of his election. The Pope's intention was very obvious: to unite all the monasteries into one Order around San Damiano and Clare. In exchange, he wanted the *sisters* of San Damiano to accept the Constitutions which he had written which were based on the Rule of St Benedict. If we look carefully at the eulogy of the *sisters* of San Damiano which follows immediately after that on Clare, we can see quite clearly that instead of giving a description of the primitive Damianite life, we are given an idealised image of a community of Poor Ladies, Recluses.

The Pope had given way before Clare's refusal to have property, and instead had granted her an extraordinary privilege: the *Privilege of Poverty*. In return, Clare had also conceded something, she had accepted the Constitutions of the *Order of San Damiano*, which had gathered monasteries of varied origins and sources into one religious family. This arrangement with Clare was obviously made under constraint, and like all such arrangements, was not destined to last.

If we now jump forward some fifteen years, we see that the picture has completely changed. In 1244 the General Chapter of the Order of Friars Minor realised the need to make a new collection of evidence about Francis in order to produce a new life of the saint. This time too—as we have noted—Thomas of Celano was charged with the task. He finished by 1247 and gave his work the title of *Memoriale Propositi*.[11] This work has more generally been known as the Second Life because it was seen as superseding his first biography.

Clare has vanished from this Second Life. Thomas of Celano does not even tell us her name. It is clear that some extremely relevant change has intervened. We see this, for instance, in Chapter X where Thomas speaks of Francis' first visit to San Damiano. In the First Life this was made the occasion to speak about Clare and the Damianites; here there is no sign of them. This silence is even more astounding when we recall that it is here, in the Second Life, that Celano speaks for the first time of the mysterious dialogue between Francis and the crucifix which he found at San Damiano, and also of the saint's prophecy about a community of women which had been made while he was repairing this little chapel. Again in Chapters 204–207, where Celano speaks of the rapport between Francis and the *sisters*, he chooses to make no mention of Clare's name. Why this silence? What has gone on between the exaltation of the First Life and the implied censure of the Second Life?

In fact Clare was not uninvolved in the tormented times that shook Francis' Order in the years immediately after his death. In 1230, soon after the encounter between Clare and Gregory IX at San Damiano, the Order held an important General Chapter in Assisi. Thomas of Eccleston tells us of a dispute between Brother Elias of Cortona and the Minister General, Crescentius of Iesi. In view of the fact that the Chapter was unable to pronounce on certain important questions which were crucial to the future of the Order itself, there must have been many such discussions. The brothers decided to appoint a commission to present these unresolved questions to the Pope. The members of this commission were all clerics, that is, chosen from the educated men. The questions to be submitted to the Pope concerned obedience to the Gospel, observance of the Testament of Francis, the use of money, poverty, the friars' houses, confession, preaching, the reception of novices to obedience, the election of the minister general and their dealings with the monasteries of women.

The Pope was happy to respond to the questions put to him by members of the Chapter, for two reasons. The first was in the political order. At San Germano, on 23 July 1230, that same year, Gregory IX had signed an important peace treaty with the Emperor Frederick II and intended to make use of the Minors to reestablish his authority, especially in certain regions of Central Italy. The second reason arose from Gregory's ties of personal friendship with Francis when he was the Cardinal Protector of the Order. Because of these ties, he considered he had a considerable and special authority over the movement born from the Poverello's preaching. The Bull *Quo elongati* of 28 September 1230, contained answers to all the questions posed. The Pope took up a position against the strict observance of the Testament of Francis. He said: 'We affirm that you are not bound to the observance of that command (of the Testament) because you cannot impose an obligation on everyone without the consensus of the brothers and above all of the ministers'.[12]

The last question put to the pope concerned the rapport with women's monasteries. The Rule forbad the friars from going into communities of women, except where they had received a special license from the Holy See. In the course of a general chapter however, held during the lifetime of Francis, the brothers were given a constitution which specified that this prohibition only concerned the monasteries of the Poor Ladies, Recluses, that is the order founded by Cardinal Hugolino. So in 1230, when the same Cardinal Hugolino, now pope, had this question put before him, he was very pleased to be able to specify that the prohibition concerned all varieties of women's religious life and that only the Apostolic See could give permission to go to these women's monasteries.

The Bull *Quo elongati* represents the first attempt at an official interpretation of Franciscan life. Numerous points dealt with there and various of the interpretations were not shared by all the brothers. For instance, we know from a letter of Peter John Olivi that towards the end to the century, some groups of the Italian brethren refused to recognise the validity of this Bull. However the larger part of the Order was well able to accept the Pope's reply for he not only spoke with the authority of the *magisterium* but also in the light of his personal friendship with Francis.

We know of one disciple of Francis who reacted strongly against the papal letter: Clare of Assisi. According to the *Legend*:

> Once when the Lord Pope Gregory forbade any brother to go to the monasteries of the Ladies without permission, the pious mother, sorrowing that her sisters would more rarely have the food of sacred teaching, sighed: 'Let him now take away from us all the brothers since he has taken away those who provide us with the food that is vital.' At once she sent back to the minister all the brothers, not wanting to have the questors who acquired corporal bread when they could not have the questors for spiritual bread. When Pope Gregory heard this, he immediately mitigated that prohibition into the hands of the general minister.[13]

The bond of friendship between Francis and Clare went back far longer than that between Francis and Hugolino/Gregory and so Clare felt herself authorised to respond to the latter. This should not stop us acknowledging the independence of the woman of Assisi which allowed her openly to contradict an explicit arrangement of the pope. As events developed, this independence of mind and action were to be manifest on other occasions too. We also see traces of it in the letters which Clare sent to one who wanted to follow her on the path of evangelical perfection, Agnes of Bohemia.

Agnes, daughter of King Ottokar I, had asked the pope if she might live, in Prague, by the same *forma vitae*, form of life, that Francis had given to Clare and her sisters. Gregory refused, saying that that text had been written for novices in the religious life and was only *potum lactis*, milky food. The true rule for the Poor Ladies, he said, was that which the pope, namely he himself, had written. Agnes wrote off to Clare asking advice and Clare replied by underlining, quite unambiguously, the value of the option for poverty:

> But because one thing is necessary, I bear witness to that one thing and encourage you, for love of Him to Whom you have offered yourself as a holy and pleasing sacrifice, that you always be mindful of your commitment like another Rachel always seeing your beginning. What you hold, may you hold, what you do, may you do and not stop. But with swift pace, light step, unswerving feet, so that even your steps stir up no dust, may you go forward securely, joyfully, and swiftly, on the path of prudent happiness, believing nothing, agreeing with nothing that would dissuade you from this commitment or would place a stumbling block for you on the way, so that nothing prevents you from offering your vows to the Most High in the perfection to which the Spirit of the Lord has called you.[14]

Without doubt, that which would 'dissuade her from this commitment' can be understood as referring to the pope himself and Clare thought it would be helpful to reinforce her own words by adding:

> In all of this, follow the counsel of our venerable father, our Brother Elias, the Minister General, that you may walk more securely in the way of the commands of the Lord. Prize it beyond the advice of the others and cherish it as dearer to you than any gift. If anyone has said anything else to you or suggested any other

thing to you that might hinder your perfection or that would seem contrary to your divine vocation, even though you must respect him, do not follow his counsel. But as a poor virgin embrace the poor Christ.[15]

With the support of Brother Elias, Clare and Agnes were in agreement about asking the pope for permission to live in Prague according to the form of evangelical poverty lived at San Damiano. This time the pope accepted Agnes's opinion and sent her a Bull which is very like the privilege of poverty which Clare had already received. None of this, however, would have helped the relationship between Clare and the pope—obviously it was no longer as it had been in the days when, still a cardinal, Hugolino had spent Easter at San Damiano.

Given this situation, perhaps we can better understand Thomas of Celano's silence about Clare in the Second Life, especially remembering that Brother Elias had been deposed in 1239. Nothing speaks louder than this silence about Clare's difficulties, even within the Franciscan movement itself.[16] We must also remember that the Second Life was a composite work. We know that it was written at request of the minister general, Crescentius of Iesi who, with a second biography of the founder in view, had asked all those who had memories of Francis to let him have them. Part of the material thus collected was used by Thomas for his Second Life and the rest is found in some unofficial compilations such as the *Legend of the Three Companions* and the so-called *Legend of Perugia*. Thus we find some passages in the Second Life which speak very negatively about relations between the brothers and women, especially about women religious, but we also find some passages which are favourable.

On rereading the Second Life, we get the impression that the same opposing positions are taken up as those adopted in the Chapter of

1230 following the Bull *Quo elongati*. In order to please everyone, Thomas of Celano inserts both pages hostile to the nuns and pages that are favourable. It would seem that Clare, even at the moment of her greatest weakness and even at the moment when she had been condemned to silence, still found ways to make her voice heard. We see an example of this in 2 Celano 204 where he says:

> The saint recognised that they were marked with many signs of the highest perfection, and that they were ready to bear any loss and undergo any labour for Christ and did not want ever to turn aside from the holy commandments. Therefore he firmly promised them and others who professed poverty in a similar way of life, that he and his brothers would perpetually offer them help and advice. And he carried this out carefully as long as he lived, and when he was close to death he commanded it to be carried out without fail always, saying that one and the same Spirit had led the brothers and those little poor ladies out of this world.[17]

This page of the Second Life corresponds exactly with Chapter VI of the Rule which Clare herself wrote about ten years later, where she says:

> When the Blessed Father saw we had no fear of poverty, hard work, trial, shame, or contempt of the world, but, instead, we held them as great delights, moved by piety he wrote a form of life for us as follows: Because by divine inspiration you have made your-selves daughters and handmaids of the most High, most Exalted King, the heavenly Father, and have taken the Holy Spirit as your spouse, choosing to live according to the perfection of the holy Gospel, I resolve and promise for myself and for my brothers always to have the same loving care and special solicitude for you as for them. As long as he lived he diligently fulfilled this and wished that it always be fulfilled by the brothers.[18]

It is true that Clare wrote after Thomas, but it is equally true that here we have a text of Francis himself, presented to us as his *ipsissima verba*, his actual words, indeed as the *forma vivendi*, the very form of life which he gave to the Damianites. Standing back for the moment, too, from the question of its authenticity, we can ask this: between 1244 and 1246, who would have made it their business to see that a text dealing with the bond between Francis and the sisters of San Damiano came into Thomas's hands? Who, if not Clare?

By the middle of the thirteenth century, then, Clare's situation had radically changed. From being so exalted in the First Life, she had passed into almost complete silence. Her name had disappeared from the official hagiographic account of Francis. Even within the Franciscan movement itself, we could say that she was not really well known. For instance, Bonaventure, when he was in Paris, only knew about her in a rather vague way, so much so that when he became minister general some years later, he had to seek information about her from Brother Leo before he could write a letter to the Poor Clares. At the same time, however, Clare was right at the heart of the Franciscan family. She and her sisters lived at San Damiano, in the very place which held the decisive memory of the blessed father's conversion when the crucifix spoke to him. The account of that dialogue began to appear in Franciscan hagiographical literature around the 1240s. It is highly likely that in this other matter too Clare and her sisters were the source of a similar diffusion of information. At the moment when any number of passages from the Second Life were putting the brethren on their guard against frequenting the women's monasteries too much, the passage about the dialogue with the crucifix reminded them that if they wanted to visit the place of Francis' conversion, then they had to go to San Damiano.

Thus San Damiano became one of the places which held

Franciscan memories. In fact there is a direct link between this primitive Franciscan place and the sources themselves, as is attested by Ubertino da Casale when he says:

> As to the testimony from heaven which this Rule received from the Lord Jesus Christ, give ear, reader, and inscribe what follows deep inside your heart. In fact it comes from the holy Brother Conrad mentioned above, who heard it directly from the holy Brother Leo who was present at the time and did the writing down of the Rule. This was done on certain scrolls in his own handwriting, and these he sent to the Monastery of Saint Clare for safe keeping as a record for the future. After all, it was on these he had written many things he had heard from the lips of the father and many things he had seen him do. Their contents cover important matters about the amazing things the saint accomplished, about the future debasement of the Rule and its subsequent revival [...] Those things Brother Bonaventure omitted on purpose, not wanting to include them in his Legend for the eyes of all [...]. But I was very sad to hear that these scrolls have been pulled apart and possibly, some missing; I was quite saddened over some of them.[19]

With the passage of time, the young, ardent and enthusiastic girl seems to have been transformed into an attentive guardian of Franciscan memories or—if you prefer—into a guardian of 'one' Franciscan memory: her own. Clare appears to have accepted the silence which descended upon her as long as her own testimony to Francis filtered out.

On the other hand, this silence was not simply something imposed from outside but was also a personal choice on the part of Clare herself. In the whole of her writings, she says not one word about her own personal life, and yet here we have a silence which speaks loudly.

Clare's choice of silence seems to have been an option for allowing the memory of Francis to speak instead. There is no missing the great number of times Clare speaks of Francis in her writings, and the complete absence of any mention of Clare in Francis' writings. Here too, one could underline the lack of symmetry.

CHAPTER
TWO

THE
CONSTRUCTION
OF A MEMORY:
THE SOURCES

The work of constructing her
memory began immediately after Clare's death, or, to put it better,
the work of constructing an image of Clare to be entrusted to history was begun. Clare was subjected to something analogous to the
construction of Francis' memory. So immediately after her death, she
became the object of this collective task, involving a number of people. Even during her funeral, Innocent IV had proposed that he celebrate the Mass for virgins and not simply for the dead. Such a
choice, put into effect even while they were transporting the body of
Clare from San Damiano to the church of San Giorgio within the
city walls, would, in fact, have meant a canonisation. However, there
was an intervention (at least according to the evidence of the *Legend*)
by the Cardinal Protector of the Order, Rainaldo, count of Jenne,
suggesting that the pope follow the procedure which had already
become the norm in the Roman Curia for a canonisation and which
expected a regular canonical procedure.

The next day the entire Curia came. The Vicar of Christ with the cardinals arrived at the place and the entire city directed its steps to San Damiano. It came time to celebrate the divine praises when, after the brothers had begun the Office of the Dead, the Lord Pope suddenly declared that the Office of Virgins should be celebrated, not that of the Dead. It seemed as though he would canonize her before placing her body in the tomb. When the most eminent Lord of Ostia replied that it would be better to proceed more slowly in these matters, the Mass of the Dead was celebrated.[20]

However, the same cardinal (at least according to the testimony of the *Legend*) was the first to reconstruct the memory of the woman of Assisi in a sermon which is now lost:

> Then, when the Supreme Pontiff with the group of prelates and cardinals was seated, the Bishop of Ostia, taking as his theme "Vanity of vanities" eulogized this outstanding woman, contemptuous of vanity, in a celebrated sermon.[21]

Thus was begun the process of reconstructing the memory of Clare. It has been noted that it was this same pope who took the first step in promoting this process. Besides the pope and men of the Curia, however, there were others who would take upon themselves this task of constructing the image of Clare. Among them, as would be logical, were first of all the *sisters* of San Damiano. Immediately after the funeral, the sisters had sent an official notice announcing the death of Clare 'to all the sisters of the Order of San Damiano who are scattered throughout the world'. It is clear that in drafting this document the sisters had had help from someone outside the monastery.[22] In spite of this, though, we can still hear the voice of the *sisters* coming through in the text, for instance:

Then, strikingly beautiful in body, rich in abundant wealth, born of noble lineage, she came to the age of marriage, when she took a poor habit for a bridal gown, a funeral for a wedding, girded herself with a rope for a wedding sash.[23]

And again:

She soothingly refreshed our hearts about the embrace of divinity, strengthening them with the antidote of continuing consolation! If she ever noticed someone in need of clothing or hungry or thirsty, she would hurry into their midst with a kind and encouraging word such as: "Bear it courteously...," "Bear the burdens of poverty patiently, the weight of humility humbly."[24]

The picture of Clare which the sisters wanted to present would not necessarily have coincided with the one which the pope wished to make known. Undoubtedly they all considered Clare a saint, but they did not all have the same idea of sanctity. This is why it is important for us today to trace the stages which led to the construction of the image of Clare which we have in the sources. The canonisation of Clare happened extremely quickly, even for the thirteenth century, in less than two years. In this period between her death and the final redaction of the *Legenda sanctae Clarae virginis*, the *Legend* or *Life of St Clare the Virgin*, there was a period during which her holiness was not only recognised and proclaimed, but also when the various pictures of the woman of Assisi which we have today, were composed and articulated until they became the memory that has been transmitted to future generations.

The Acts of the Canonisation Process
The pope had not abandoned the idea of officially canonizing Clare of Assisi. Therefore, he had hardly returned to Anagni when he wrote

a letter to Bartolomeo Accorombani, Archbishop of Spoleto, in which he set in motion the regular process leading to a canonisation.[25] Bartolomeo (who also had civil jurisdiction over Assisi at that time) chose some officials to help him in this informational phase, then selected some men of religion, which would guarantee the regular evolution of the process, and then a notary to make a proper record of the replies of those questioned. On 24 November, 1253, barely three and a half months after the death of Clare, the first session of the process was held in the cloister of San Damiano, in the presence of this same Bartolomeo, Archbishop of Spoleto, of the archdeacon Leonardo and the archpriest of Trevi, Giacomo, of Brother Mark, visitator of the sisters of San Damiano, two of the faithful companions of Francis—Angelo and Leo—and finally of the notary Martino.

A canonisation process ends, obviously, with the final acceptance of the candidate to the glories of the altar. To this end, those commissioned with the task of making the inquiry were furnished with a schema for questioning, designed to avoid useless digressions on the part of the witnesses. Although we do not have the 'questions' which the pope, Innocent IV, named in his letter to Archbishop Bartolomeo when he initiated the process, we can clearly see from the words of all the witnesses that they were responding within a single schema. This was in fact indicated in the initial letter, namely: her *life* in her father's house; her *conversion* or choice of religious life; then her *conversation*, meaning her conduct during the years at San Damiano, and finally the *miracles*, those divine signs confirming her holiness.

Each testimony was put into Latin by the notary because it would be used at the canonisation. Within a few days, a number of witnesses would be interviewed, among them fifteen sisters of San Damiano, a woman who had been Clare's friend since childhood and four men from Assisi, of whom one, the last, had been a servant in her father's household. Normally, the Acts of the process of canonisation were not kept once they had led to the actual proclamation of the candidate's sanctity and been used in writing the official *Legenda*, or Life. For this reason it was accepted for many years that the Acts of Clare's process were lost. They were only rediscovered at the beginning of the twentieth century, in a translation in the Umbrian dialect dating from the 1400s, in a single manuscript now preserved in the Biblioteca Nazionale of Florence.[26] It is clear that we are dealing here with first hand material which still retains the immediacy of the spoken word, even though it has twice been translated (the evidence would have been given in the local dialect and translated into Latin, then this was translated into the version we know today).

The Bull of Canonisation: "Clara claris praeclara"

The canonisation process was virtually over by the 29 November 1253. The actual canonisation of Clare in Anagni did not take place, however, until somewhere between August and October 1255. Why this delay, especially in the light of the urgency which Innocent IV showed immediately after Clare's death? At the heart of this lies the rupture of relations between the Friars Minor and the pope, a rupture caused by the dispute at the University of Paris between the secular masters and the mendicants.[27] It is possible that in this polemical atmosphere, Innocent delayed proclaiming a saint someone like Clare who was in the front rank of the minorite movement. A short time later, Innocent died and was succeeded by that same Rainaldo who had recommended prudence at the funeral, the one who had been cardinal protector of the Order and who knew Clare personally. Rainaldo, who took the name of Alexander IV, hastened to nullify the decision against the Minors.[28]

The Bull of Canonisation for Clare, *Clara claris praeclara,* was promulgated by Alexander IV in the cathedral at Anagni at the beginning of autumn of 1255. It has been written of this document that

> the bull is a good example of the transformation in pontifical documents of this type, which took place in the years after Innocent IV. They are no longer mere rhetorical exercises but they take account, admittedly in a rarefied literary form, of events with a more concrete pastoral focus. The narrative about the life of the saint and his/her virtues thus becomes the principal part and centre of the document.'[29]

In other words, even in a document as clearly focussed as a bull of canonisation, the real woman and the story of her life can still be discovered behind the saint whose cultus the bull is supposedly promoting, even though this life be interpreted in the light of the pontifical pastoral preoccupations. What exactly were these preoccupations?

The whole of the first part of the bull 'is a play on the motif of *claritas,* clarity or light, used by the pope as a synonym for holiness, developed and interwoven from time to time with the theme of *claritas* as fame and excellence. Exalting the luminosity of Clare carries the pope to confront that which had from the start seemed the 'paradox' of Clare: how reconcile this exaltation of her visible and luminous qualities of which the fame as so widespread, with the contrary idea of the culture of the period that feminine virtue was allied to modesty, to hiddenness, to silence and to invisibility?'[30]

From the literary point of view, this response is extremely beautiful:

> O how great is the vibrancy of this light and how intense is the brilliance of its illumination! While this light remained certainly in a hidden enclosure, it emitted sparkling rays outside. Placed in the confined area of the monastery, yet she was spread throughout the

wide world. Hidden within, she extended herself abroad. Yes, Clare hid, yet her life has come to light. Clare was silent yet her fame was proclaimed. She was hidden in a cell but known in cities.[31]

And saying this, the pope indeed made of Clare a 'light remaining within a hidden enclosure' *(lux secretis inclusa claustralibus)*. Yet this too was an image of Clare, and one which was to have great success in the centuries ahead.

The Legend of Saint Clare the Virgin

The work of constructing the memory of Clare could not be called conclusively finished even with her canonisation. The official Life also had to be written, the *Legend,* which means—as the word implies—a text to be read (*legere* in Latin). This *Legend* would be aimed at making the new saint known to all Christians. Alexander IV, therefore, commissioned a cleric who was skilled in this type of writing and he brought his task to a conclusion in short order. Thus was born the *Legend of Saint Clare the Virgin,* a most important document if we are to learn the biographic profile of Clare of Assisi, and of course until the rediscovery of the Acts of the Canonisation Process, this was almost our only source for her life.

Before we can approach such a text, there are a few points which need to be noted. The first concerns the author. In 1910, Francesco Pennacchi, the modern editor of the *Legenda,* attributed it to Thomas of Celano, placing the prologue to this text side by side with the *Vita Prima* and concluding:

> Either Celano is the author of our Legend or it was written by one
> of his brethren who had studied Celano's work for so long that he
> had wonderfully assimilated both his opinions and his defects.[32]

In fact, Codex 338 of the Commune Library in Assisi (and now in the library of the Sacro Convento) makes no mention of the author and therefore some people have had reservations about making any such attribution. The name of Thomas of Celano only appeared on the stage in the fifteenth century in an anonymous compilation of a *Life of Saint Clare* which drew on all the known sources and which says:

> The prelate Innocent IV having paid the debt of human nature, Rainaldo, Cardinal and Protector of the Order, was elevated to the papacy. It was he who inscribed this most holy woman in the catalogue of holy virgins and commanded the holy Brother Thomas of Celano, who had been the companion and disciples of Saint Francis, that he should write the radiant memorial of this virgin Clare. He had already written the first life of the blessed father Francis, at the command of Pope Gregory IX. Now, like a son of obedience, he wrote the Legend of this same blessed Clare in an elegant and ordered style. However, he did not put into the Legend everything which had been contained in the Process conducted by Bartolomeo, Bishop of Spoleto.[33]

The second point to be made concerns the type of literature which we call hagiography. When you want to make use of a hagiographic text, it is always wise to specify the difference between hagiographical and historical writing. In general, hagiography has its own characteristics which must be noted if we are to interpret and indeed appreciate it properly. Above all this would be true of its purpose or end. While history seeks the truth of an incident, hagiography desires the edification, or building up, of the reader or, to put it better, hagiography too seeks the truth but its concept of truth is different from that of modern history. For this reason, while history is particularly attentive to the moments of beginning and ending, hagiography starts by looking at what is ongoing in the incident, to a progressive revelation of holiness. Secondly, it looks to the beginning. Every hagiographic text is intimately connected to the milieu, the group, the context which produced it. The saint is *thus* in the memory of the group of disciples or of the faithful which promotes this remembrance and their memory is not simply the remembering of a person. It is also—and always—the presentation of a model, a mirror, a foundational example of a style of life. This 'place' can partly be the same as the 'place' for which the text is destined; in the case of religious orders, for instance, the community of men or women which has produced the text wants to perpetuate it within the community of readers in future generations. Things shift with time, of course, and hagiographic texts have a double movement: on the one hand they represent a certain standing back from the moment of origin; on the other, they indicate a journey of return to that same origin.

In this sense the *Legenda sanctae Clarae virginis* is a typical product of the *genre* of literary hagiography of the thirteenth century. This hagiography of Clare also has as its purpose, to promote the edification of the listener (since a *Legenda* was, in fact, written to be read aloud). Its context or environment was the monastery of San Damiano and its destination the numerous forms of women's religious life scattered throughout Europe. Similarly, while the work takes a certain distance from Clare and her disciples, it is also destined to preserve her as a beautiful icon, but an inaccessible one.

When compared with other similar compilations, what makes the *Legenda sanctae Clarae virginis* particularly interesting to the modern historian is the fact we also have preserved for us the Acts of the canonisation process, in other words the main source on which the author of the *Legend* based his work. This enables us to examine these two sources in the light of each other, and thus have more insight into the hagiographer's way of working.

At the beginning of the Legend, in the introductory letter addressed to the pope, the author explains his method of working and the circumstances through which he began his task:

> It has obviously pleased Your Lordship to command my lowliness to mold from the recent deeds of Saint Clare, a text to be read aloud. I would certainly dread this task because of my ignorance of writing except that the papal authority has again and again placed it before me. Therefore placing myself at your command, I did not consider it safe to proceed with what might be incomplete, resorted to the companions of blessed Francis and to the community of Christ's virgins, and turned over and again in my heart that axiom: no-one should write history except those who have seen it or received it from those who have.[34]

The biographer knew well that in 'ancient times' it was not considered legitimate to write history except on the basis of eyewitness testimonies. This was following the example of numerous masters so that he not only based his work on the Acts of the Canonisation Process but also on the testimony of some companions of Francis[35] as well as the companions of Clare who had lived with her at San Damiano.

The 'modernity' (for the thirteenth century) of this approach consisted precisely in the search for the truth and this remained the ground of the work which the author intended to produce. This does not mean to say that the *Legenda sanctae Clarae virginis* is to be read as an historical biography in the contemporary understanding of that term. The author wanted to spur the reader on to holiness and not simply to recount the story of Clare of Assisi. With this in view, therefore, he thought that the truth would be the best guarantee of the efficacy of his relating. It is precisely this which constitutes his 'modernity'.

In a situation which is rare in the history of medieval sources, we today can now read one source (*Legenda sanctae Clarae virginis*) together with its own source. It is a kind of game of Chinese boxes in which one source contains the other. Reading the *Legend* and the Acts of the Canonisation Process in the light of each other, allows us to see just how an official biography could be substantially sincere in its declaration of fidelity to the sources. All the content of the *Legend* derives from the Process, and almost everything in the Process later reappears in the *Legend*. However, there are some interesting discrepancies between the sources, discrepancies which arise from the culture and spiritual sensitivities of the author. All these will be considered in the pages which follow. Before proceeding with that, though, we need to sharpen our focus on some other observations concerning the authorship of the *Legenda* and which have already emerged from the dedicatory letter. The first thing to note is that the author is a man, an ecclesiastic who shares with his contemporaries in a vague prejudice against women. The second thing to note is that the author is a theologian, indeed a good one, but this work demands that he uses non-theological language (and this is one of the characteristics of hagiographic literature).

With regard to his anti-woman prejudice, the hagiographer presents it as utterly normal. In fact, in the same dedicatory letter, after having explained how a merciful God met the needs of the world by sending Francis and Dominic as leaders of the way and teachers of life, then adds:

> It was not fitting that help be lacking for the more fragile sex, caught in the maelstrom of passion, which no less a desire drew to sin and no greater frailty impelled.[36]

With this perspective, the fragility which belongs to the 'weaker sex' was to be understood also in the moral sense. Women were naturally more inclined to sin than men, and this view of our author would not only have been that of all men but also of all women too. If the biographer underlined this sexual, moral and theological fragility in his introduction to the *Legend*, this not only reflected the general mindset but was also a means whereby he could throw the value of Clare's holiness into greater relief. She succeeded in becoming so holy *in spite of* being a woman. This attitude is certainly not confined to the thirteenth century.

With regard to the apparently non-theological language of the *Legend*, we must remember that the function of hagiography included drama as well as instruction. Above all the *Legend* was a text designed to be read in the refectory during meals or at times of monastic 'recreation'. This makes it quite different from a theological or an exegetical work. Hagiography always seeks to be a good experience. The ingenuity of each story is nothing other than the unexpected overturning of the ordinary by the events of another dimension. On more than one page the hagiographer of Clare reveals a certain level of awareness of popular religion which in itself reveals that he belongs to a world of more cultured religion. This explains his attitude, which we have already mentioned, towards women, beginning indeed with those very religious for whom he intended his work. He admits, in fact, to having written in a very simple style:

> I then set it down in a simple style [so] that it will delight the virgins to read about the wonders of the virgin and my uncultivated intelligence will not fall upon the ignorant where it might be unintelligible by reason of an excess of words.[37]

However there is no need for us to be deceived: hagiography in general and the *Legenda sanctae Clarae virginis* in particular is never ingen-

uous, even when it displays some naïve traits. Behind episodes which
apparently serve only to make us smile, there is always, more or less
hidden, the mind of a theologian. In the same way, apparently
insignificant omissions are, as often as not, motivated by serious theological considerations.

What then is the span of the image of Clare which we can take
from the *Legend*? Stefano Brufani has made this reply:

> It seems to me that this image is strongly marked by the model of
> monastic holiness into which the biographer has conscientiously
> tried to fit the experience of Clare. The novelty which was minor-
> ity does not shine through. Clare, in the reconstruction of her
> hagiography (and perhaps even in reality) is still tied to the tradi-
> tional monasticism of the preceding centuries. And the presence of
> Francis is only that—a presence.[38]

Here the work of constructing a hagiographic memory comes to its
conclusion. Here must begin the work of history in the modern
sense of the term, which consists precisely in the dismantling of the
sources (the expression belongs to Marc Bloch) in order, as far as possible, to reconcile the disparity between the hagiographic reconstruction and the reality.

The Writings of Clare

It is impossible to end this chapter on the sources for Clare of Assisi
without at least a quick glance at her own writings.[39] In fact, women
of the Middle Ages seem to have been silent because history is written by those in command. Therefore all the sources which speak
about women in the Middle Ages were in fact written by men, and
by men who on the whole, as we have already seen, did not hide their
prejudices. We can count on one hand the number of women who,
by means of their writings, have made their voices echo through the

ages until today. Clare is one of these rare women who have broken through this wall of silence. We have several writings attributed to her, some with certitude (the Rule for example) and some with good reason (the four letters sent to Agnes of Bohemia) and some with a question mark (the Testament and the Blessing) In each case, her 'voice' did not die with her, in spite of the fact that she was a woman of a particular culture and that she lived for more than forty years enclosed behind four walls. Even if someone did not want to believe in her holiness, they must believe that this is a small 'historical miracle' of the woman of Assisi.

• • •

CHAPTER
THREE

COURTESY

Ioanni de Ventura spoke under oath about these matters and said he, the witness, used to converse in Saint Clare's house while she was still a young girl and a virgin in her father's house because he was a house watchman. Lady Clare could then have been eighteen or so and of the most noble stock of all Assisi, on both her father's and her mother's side. Her father was called Favarone and her grandfather Offreduccio de Bernardino. The young girl at that time was of such an upright life and dress, as if in the monastery for a long time.

> Asked what sort of life she led, he replies: although their house-
> hold was one of the largest in the city and great sums were spent
> there, she nevertheless saved the food they were given to eat, put
> it aside and then sent it to the poor.[40]

All the witnesses whose testimony has been preserved for us were either sisters of Clare at San Damiano or key people in the society of Assisi. Only Ioanni de Ventura, the final witness, did not belong to either category since he was a servant. His evidence, however, was so valuable that both the notary and the fourteenth century translator thought it necessary to insert it with the other evidence. The reason why it was so important is obvious: Ioanni had known Clare since she was a small child and as a young girl ('a young girl and a virgin'). He also knew her well since he was a domestic servant, a man of the household, a 'fameglio' which means that he was a member of the wider extended family in a way which was typical of the Middle Ages.

In a few words he gives us an exact picture of the social standing of Clare's family. All the words he uses have what we might almost call a 'technical' meaning, beginning from the title he reserves for Clare calling her 'Madonna' meaning 'my lady'. This was the title reserved for aristocratic women. In Latin the word *Domina* means 'lady' and is the term used to designate the lady who is head of the family, the mistress of the servants. In the Italian, the word modulated until it came finally to mean any woman who was married. In the thirteenth century, however, *Madonna*, with its masculine equivalent of *messere* is the title reserved to women to whom one pays respect—as Clare was for Ioanni de Ventura. And we see that he immediately adds that Madonna Clare was 'of the most noble stock of all Assisi, on both her father's side and her mother's.' For Ioanni it was important to underline that her nobility was on her mother's side as well as her father's in order to indicate that Clare had four quarterings of nobility. However his attention returns at once to her father's side for this was the more indicative of nobility. Here Ioanni gives the names of her father, grandfather and great grandfather—Favorone di Offreduccio di Bernadino—and by so doing he is tracing her nobility back for a hundred years at least. His precision is one of many signs indicating the care with which an aristocratic family safeguarded the record of its lineage.

Ioanni then adds: the court (or household) was one of the largest in the city.[41] The household (*corte*) is not used by chance. The *court* certainly signified the inner courtyard of the signorial palace (in this case a fortified palace which was the town residence of an aristocratic family) but it had come to mean all the inhabitants of the palace, all those who lived beneath its roof. In this sense, the *corte* or household was, for Ioanni, synonymous with the family, and also the extended family which included all the various dependants of the head of the family and also all the men and women servants and the men of arms who made that household their headquarters. The old servant is proud to have been part of all that, as we see when he mentions the abundant food given by Clare 'as in a great household'. In Assisi, not everyone could enjoy such an abundance of food and for Ioanni de Ventura, it was a privilege to have been a servant in such a grand house. He had already specified that the household was one of the greatest in the city. This does not only mean that Clare's family was one of the most important families in Assisi. 'Greatest' *(maggiori)* here is an Italian translation of the Latin *maiores*. The court of Favarone di Offreduccio belonged to that defined group of aristocratic families which, in Assisi, made up the *maiores* as opposed to the *minores*, or *ordinary people*. There were about twenty families who had any sort of power base in the area but who, during the course of the twelfth century, became urbanised and part of the tapestry of the city. For the most part, they built their houses on the high ground, around the Cathedral of San Rufino. At the end of the twelfth century there was a true civil war waged against these families. The *maggiori* were driven into exile and from that exile, stirred up the rivals of Perugia to make war on Assisi. Finally, they came home and were part of the peace treaty of 1205 and later of 1210. At the time of which Ioanni is testifying, the members of aristocratic families were perfectly inserted into the structure of the commune, and occupied prestigious positions in the magistrature of Assisi. And so it was with pride that in his witness, Ioanni de Ventura specifies that *Madonna* Clare, the Lady Clare, came from the most noble families of the city of Assisi. What did this tell us about a young girl growing up in a noble family in the thirteenth century? How did an aristocratic child live? In this sense, the Acts of the Canonisation Process are an interesting source. When Ioanni di Ventura speaks about the 'court' of the descendants of Offreduccio, he is referring to that whole aristocratic world which spread from Aquitaine throughout all Europe and which quickly developed into what became known as the 'courtly culture'.

The family of Clare belonged to that world. This was underlined during the canonisation process by the other men witnesses who themselves came from that same aristocratic background. For instance, Messer Pietro di Damiano said that:

> he, and his father lived near Saint Clare's house and that of her father and other members of her family. He knew Lady Clare when she was in the world and knew her father, Lord Favarone, who was noble, great and powerful in the city—he and the others of his household. Lady Clare was noble, of a noble family and of an upright manner of life. There were seven knights of her household, all of whom were noble and powerful.'[42]

Here we meet the term 'knight' which to all those listening clearly defined the social condition of Clare's father.

> Little by little, throughout the tenth century, there developed a vocabulary which, especially in France, became the distinctive mark of all the aristocracy. In its Latin form, these terms express the military vocation, while popular speech, with more accuracy, used the term 'knight' for all those who, from the backs of their war-horses, dominated the poor and terrorized the monks. It was their arms and their warlike attitudes which united them.[43]

By using the word *knight*, the witness places Clare's family very exactly within that traditional three-part division of medieval society into *oratores, bellatores et laboratores*, prayers, fighters and workers.

Towards the end of the ninth century and developing during the tenth so that it became commonplace by the twelfth, there appeared in medieval literature a tendency to describe society by three categories and orders. According to the classic formula of Adalberone di Laon, who lived at the start of the eleventh century, the three components of the tripartite society were: *oratores, bellatores, laboratores*, that is clerics, fighters and workers.'[44]

The thinking behind this threefold division of society was extremely simple. God had given each man a specific task: some had the mission of praying for the salvation of all, others were dedicated to fighting in order to protect the multitude of people, and by their work the members of the third group, by far the more numerous, were expected to support both the men of the Church and the men of war. This scheme which rapidly imposed itself on the collective awareness, presented an extremely simple model, in conformity with the divine plan and thereby ratifying social inequalities and all kinds of economic barrenness. The vocation of men in the second order, the *bellatores*,

> was war; and the primary use that they made of their wealth was the acquisition of more effective means of combat. [...] The horse became the principal weapon of the combatant and the symbol of his superiority, to the extent that these warriors became known as the *cavalieri* (men on horseback)'.[45]

For many centuries these violent men, the knights, left anything cultural in the hands of the clerics. It is well known that even the Great Charlemagne had difficulty in reading and writing. However, in the eleventh century, radiating from an area on the edge of Europe, from Aquitaine, there developed a cultural movement which had precisely these knights as its focus.

Towards 1100, from a count of Poitiers, Duke of Aquitaine, emerge the first love songs which have come down to us. To Gregorian melodies he fitted words eulogizing his lady. He was at once imitated by all the young men of his court. Thus was born the game of love, in which the lover, longing for the wife of his lord, transferred to her the devotion, the attitudes and the obligations of the vassal. The ways of courtly love were elaborated by an aristocracy to which the Church, enclosed in her cloisters and absorbed in her litanies of redemption, exercised little enough restraint on the inspiration north of the Loire and which spread rapidly into the areas around Toulouse, Provence and finally Italy.[46]

In this way the so-called courtly-knightly culture was born. It roots were to be found in the d'Oc language, but it swiftly leapt over the narrow confines of this to become a culture of everyday life with codes of conduct and ideals of life. The knightly ideal is at once a social fact and a literary reality. The poetic imagination assumed the stature of a model, an example, it imposed rules of behaviour, it looked upwards towards an ever higher aspiration and awareness which, until then, had been only latent and confused. The knightly ideal was a turning point in the history of civilization.

It is very interesting to see just how a violent and warlike society was able to bring forth an ideal as elevated as this one. Reflected in it were the aspiration and ideals which the free people of the Germanic tribes had cultivated for centuries: love of danger, courage, solidarity in time of war. For centuries these ideals had also been found in the Latin culture and in the Christian message. The knightly-courtly culture was born from a meeting of all these, and the knightly ideal represents a transfiguration of the hard reality of war as it was found among its protagonists. This was how the spirit of love for danger became a spirit of broad generosity, of greatness of heart, of a desire to pour out one's life in service of a great ideal.

During the years when Clare was a young girl, the courtly romances were spreading from court to court, telling stories of knights who lost their lives in pursuit of the Grail. Solidarity in war, that necessary bond between a group of armed men, was transfigured into loyalty with its solemn task to remain faithful to one's word once given. Thus the courtly ideal constructed a network of living fidelities which even allowed for communication between enemies. The knight was, in fact, not only bound to be faithful to his word at the risk of receiving the most damning of accusations, that of 'fellonia'— 'treason', but the knight was also bound to believe in the word of another, at least until proved untrustworthy. Finally, courage became distinguished from indifference. The knight did not act only in his own interests. Indeed, even when confronted with the middle class society and the new social classes to which this gave rise, the knightly ideal managed to deepen these elements. It was the merchant who turned all to his own advantage; not so the knight who demonstrated his power precisely in the liberality of giving without measure. The clergy were well aware of this and in the Handbooks for Confessors (which were being developed at this time) they explained that the sin of the nobility was not greed but pride.

We find that the theme of love is central to the values of the courtly-knightly culture from the thirteenth century onwards. We have heard about 'courtly love' which has been hailed as one of the greatest 'inventions' of the Middle Ages. It was of just this love that someone was able to write about 'love, this invention of the XII century'.[47] It is not that there was no love before this date, only that the

Latin word *amor* was mainly used for the male sexual appetite, and for affection the softer term *dilectio* was preferred. In courtly poetry, however, love, *amor*, becomes an elevated feeling which could not only overwhelm a man sensually but also impel him towards the most high thoughts.

It has been said concerning this courtly love, that is it a paradoxical love since it is a love which longs for possession but which grows in a state of non-possession. It is love from afar off which contains, at the same time, the desire truly to touch the lady even while chastity itself keeps him far from her. Whatever interpretation we choose to give to this love, or better to this loving paradox, the fact remains that it represents a breach in the fabric of medieval culture, and woman, the great absentee from the culture of the preceding centuries now finds herself for good or ill, taking the centre stage.'

'The great culture of the XI century ignored women and even art allowed them little space. There are no figures of women saints or if there are, they are more like idols of gold with wasp eyes staring into the edges of the darkness, and whose absent gaze no-one dares break. [...] The world of knights was a masculine society, [...] the greatest knightly virtues were courage and strength, boldness and aggression.'[48]

In the literature of this knightly-courtly culture, on the other hand, woman is the focus of all poetry, the centre of all attention. Indeed, two things must not be forgotten: the first is that courtly love is constructed from the man's perspective, even if from the viewpoint of a man who places himself in a position of inferiority. The woman owes her elevation to him, and only to him, and if she does not treat her servant appropriately, then every time, she risks the loss of all. The second thing to remember is that courtly culture as it is presented to us today in the sources is only a literary creation. For this reason it would be dangerous to believe these documents cast a direct light on any lived reality. This is not to say, on the other hand, that such literature had no influence on life in the concrete. On the contrary, the courtly ideal elaborated the rules and models of behaviour which widely influenced the social life of the thirteenth century.

While the virtues demanded of men were, as we have seen, courage, fidelity and strength, those required of women were of quite another character. As has been neatly expressed by Guy de Couey:

On n'aime pas dame por parenté,
Mais quant elle est belle et cortoise et sage.[49]
(One does not love a woman for her lineage
but because she is beautiful, courteous and wise.)

Beauty, courtesy and wisdom: These were the attributes demanded of a true courtly woman.

It is exactly beauty, courtesy and good reputation that were the attributes unanimously given to Clare in the testimonies of the Canonisation Process. Her good reputation was singled out above all by the women who gave evidence. They stressed that throughout her youth, Clare's behaviour—or, as they said, her 'conversation'—was always honest. 'Honestas' in Latin means honourable or respectable. For example, Cristiana de Bernardo affirms that 'in the house of her father, she was considered by everyone to be upright and holy.'[50] Pacifica di Guelfuccio says: Madonna Clare was 'considered by all those who knew her to be of great honesty and of very good life.'[51]

For a young aristocratic woman, this *honestas*, this integrity, was not only important socially but it was also an interior disposition. In other words, we are not only talking about rejoicing in a good reputation but about maturing in that wisdom considered appropriate to the courtly lady and which was called prudence. It is this prudence which emerges from an exceptional witness: Bona di Guelfuccio, sister of Pacifica and childhood friend of Clare. While her sister later followed Clare to San Damiano, Bona married, but at the time of the Process, she was called to give evidence because of the intimacy which had bound her to Clare from childhood. She testified therefore, saying:

> At the time she entered religion, she was a prudent girl of eighteen years. She had always stayed in the house, hidden, not wanting to be seen by those who passed in front of her house. She was also very kind and took care of all other good deeds. Asked how she knew the things spoken of, she replied: because she used to converse with her.[52]

Bona then 'conversava' that is she used to converse with Clare and therefore knew well the habits of this 'prudent young woman'. The picture she describes is a fragment of thirteenth century daily life. Clare's home was in the piazza next to the cathedral of San Rufino. This was one of the two piazzas of the city (the other was that of the market place which today we call the Piazza Commune). It was here, around sunset that, in all probability, the young and not so young met to talk. Women rarely came out into the piazza, and aristocratic young women almost never. The bourgeois women went to the market during the day or to conduct business in the various shops. Aristocratic women could not go out of their palaces unless they were accompanied by an *honest companion*. What some probably did, even among the aristocracy, was to stand in the window and allow themselves to be admired by whoever was passing by. This was accepted behaviour even if considered less than prudent. Clare, however, demonstrated her own prudence in this matter by keeping herself back from the glances of strangers.

Here, it seems, we must look at a literary model—who could fail
to think of Dante's Beatrice?

> So deeply to be reverenced, so fair,
> My lady is when she her smile bestows,
> All sound of speaking falters to a close
> And eyes which would behold her do not dare.
> Of praises sung of her she is aware
> Yet clad in sweet humility she goes.
> A thing from Heaven sent, to all she shows
> A miracle in which the world may share.[53]

Clare, like Beatrice, was honest, that is honourable and polite, kind,
and for this reason, humbly kept herself from the staring of strangers.

The second characteristic of Clare, after prudence and good reputation, was courtesy. Here the witnesses use a whole series of adjec-
tives which could be seen as synonyms. Clare was *gentle* and *kind*. The
Latin word *gentiles* indicates those who belong to the same *gens*, the
same race, the same family. By the thirteenth century the word had
come to mean the manner in which those of 'good family' would
therefore behave. Thus gentleness is the most typical attribute of an
aristocratic lady and is the synonym of courtesy. The same can be said
of kindness, *benignitas*. The word is made up of *bene* (good) and *gignere*
which means to generate, and so *benignitas* indicates 'one who is of
good birth and good nature'.

It is interesting to see how a violent, and in some respects primitive, world like that of Europe in the thirteenth century, had been
able 'invent' courtesy and gentleness and how these were part of a
system of lay values, even though they were greatly influenced by the
message of the gospel. Courtesy and gentleness did not call the social
roles into question at all. The gentle knight who took up the defence
of the weak did not thereby renounce his strength but simply used

it in favour of those weak. In the same way, the courteous lady who graciously gave herself to the works of mercy, did not thereby bring her aristocratic *status* in question. Her graciousness was shown all the more but did not undermine it. We are a long way from: if you wish to be perfect, go and sell what you have and give it to the poor, and then come, follow me'. Graciousness and courtesy are not the same as Gospel love for our enemies or pardon for sinners. But, precisely because they are lay qualities, courtesy and graciousness represent great human values. Graciousness is that attitude of doing everything without wanting things to be different. The courteous lady treats everyone graciously not because she hopes to receive something in return, but simply because this reveals the nobility of her soul. All the witnesses at the Process are in agreement here, that Clare was a young woman of courtesy, graciousness and kindness. Benvenuta of Perugia says:

> She was a virgin in spirit and body and held in great veneration by all who knew her even before she entered religion.[54]

and Messer Ugolino di Pietro Girardone says:

> This Saint Clare was a virgin of a very upright manner of life in her father's house, and was kind and gracious to everyone.[55]

Pietro di Damiano:

> The Lady Clare was noble, of a noble family and of an upright manner of life.[56]

The third of Clare's qualities which the process highlights is her beauty. It is not a coincidence that the one who speaks of this is a man. He does it almost in passing, speaking of the problem of her marriage:

> Because she had a beautiful face, a husband was considered for her.
> Many of her relatives begged her to accept them as a husband but
> she never wanted to consent.[57]

This detail about her beauty has no interest for the author of the
Legend nor for the sisters at San Damiano but it makes us understand
the interest of an aristocratic male like Ranieri di Bernardo, for
beauty was one of the qualities required of a courtly lady. The one
who is speaking is a man who had known Clare since she was a
young girl in her father's house. His wife was her cousin so he was
well informed of the facts. It is interesting that he was so well able to
remember her beauty but even more interesting that he linked that
beauty to the problem of her marriage, More than that, he himself
was involved in that problem:

> Since the witness himself had many times asked her to be willing
> to consent to this, she did not even want to hear him; moreover
> she preached to him of despising the world.[58]

This introduces a new element. Up to this point, Clare as we find her
in the witnesses' testimony, appears as a young aristocratic woman
brought up according to the canons of the courtly culture: she was
beautiful, kind and prudent. There was every indication that she
would have consented to the prospects put before her. As the witnesses say: They spoke of finding her a husband. This was because the
choice of a husband for her was something which concerned the
whole family. In the end, marriage was nothing but an alliance of two
'lines' ratified by an exchange of gifts: the woman and the dowry.

Certainly in the century before Clare, the Church had struggled
hard to promote a different idea of matrimony, in opposition to this
aristocratic one, but the fruits of that struggle were still too recent to
have entered into the ordinary customs of the time. The Church had

insisted strongly that the ministers of the sacrament of matrimony were the two being married, that is the man and the woman. A valid marriage required the full and free consent of the woman. This was the first time in the history of civilization that this principle was so strongly affirmed. Throughout the history of civilization, marriages had been made by the bridegroom with the father of the bride or a male member of her family. Only in the most civilised period of Roman history was legislation introduced requiring the consent of the bride and even here there was a triple consent: the bridegroom, the father of the bride and finally that of the bride herself. Christian marriage, as it was defined more and more precisely during the course of the twelfth century, was the first family institution in which the two partners were placed absolutely level—at least juridically. It was not so in the Germanic tradition nor was it the custom among West European aristocracy. Marriage was, above all, a bond of two lines and was designed to maintain the blood line. In cases of sterility, it was always the woman who ran the risk of repudiation whether the sterility was hers or only presumed to be hers.

The knightly classes had to cede to the clerical here, and, in practice, accept the new idea of matrimony, but affirmation of the principle that the woman's consent was necessary did not make her consent certain in practice. In thirteenth-century Italy it was practically impossible for a young aristocratic girl like Clare to choose the companion of her life. One result of the Church's struggle, however, was that while the woman may not have the liberty to say who she would like to marry, she did have the liberty to refuse a husband.

This is exactly what happened with Clare. Various husbands were proposed to her, but she had the liberty to refuse them all. The evidence underlines that Clare was eighteen years old which was late to marry. Normally young women were promised in marriage while they were children and marriages generally celebrated when they were between fourteen and eighteen years old. If Clare, at eighteen, was not yet promised to anyone, then this means that her resistance to the matrimonial project of the family had begun some while previously.

This is the breaking point in the biographical account of the lady of Assisi. Messer Raniero di Bernardo said that Clare herself invited him to 'despise the world'. The young noble woman was certainly looking beyond the knightly-courtly ideal to something else, something which she had already made her own. To 'despise the world' is a technical expression, not part of the knightly-courtly culture but the language of religion and penance.

CHAPTER
FOUR

CONVERSION

Francis, in his Testament, had said:

The Lord gave me, Brother Francis, thus to begin doing penance
in this way: for when I was in sin, it seemed too bitter for me to
see lepers. And the Lord himself led me among them and I showed
mercy to them. And when I left them, what had seemed bitter to
me was turned to sweetness of soul and body. And afterwards I
delayed a little and left the world.[59]

'To leave the world' was the expression used, even by Francis, to
indicate conversion. By the thirteenth century this expression carried a long history. In every hagiographical legend, in every life of a
saint, conversion represented one of the most important transition
points. The model for every Legend or Life, was the Life of St
Anthony, father of the desert monks, which had been written by
Athanasius, Metropolitan of Alexandria in the fourth century. In
this, he recounts how Anthony, left an orphan with a much younger
sister, went, one day,

into the church and at that moment heard the Lord say to the rich
young man: If you would be perfect, go and sell what you own and

give to the poor, and you will have treasure in heaven, then come and follow me.' Anthony, as if this reading had been made for him, immediately left the church, sold his goods and distributed the considerable proceeds to the poor, keeping back only a modest income for his sister. Going again in to the church, he heard the Lord say in the Gospel: Give no thought to the morrow. Unable to stay in the church, he went out at once and gave the poor whatever remained. He entrusted his sister to some virgins he knew who would educate her in virginity. For himself, then, he left his house and devoted himself to asceticism, living most austerely.[60]

Anthony left his city, Alexandria, and retired to pray in the desert. This was the beginning of monasticism. His example was to be followed by thousands upon thousands of monks and nuns throughout the centuries.

In the hagiographic legends of key monastic figures, conversion was the moment when a life was changed. It was a moment of particular importance because it indicated a new birth into a life of holiness, according to the command of the Lord to Nicodemus: Unless one is born of water and the Holy Spirit, one cannot enter the Kingdom of Heaven.[61] Even physically this coincides with the moment of leaving the world. The person abandons their own family and their own home in order to live an eremitical life in the desert or forest, or indeed to live a cenobitic life in a monastic community. However, during the Middle Ages, when there was such an affirmation in the West of the cenobitic life, conversion ended up by meaning much the same as 'entering into religion'. This means, canonically, abandoning *lay* status and acquiring that of the religious or monastic.

This scheme, developed through monastic hagiographies, ran into difficulties when speaking about saints who did not enter monastic life or choose religious life itself. The outstanding example of this is Francis of Assisi himself. It is extremely hard to specify the exact moment when his conversion happened. Most probably we are dealing here with a long inner struggle which, by means of various attempts, brought him to recognise just what his vocation was to be. The monastic hagiographic schema which saw conversion as a precise event, had to be pulled out of shape by the first biographers.

Thomas of Celano, in his *First Life* of Francis, speaks in this way about his conversion:

> The hand of the Lord was upon him, a change of the right hand of the Most High, that through him the Lord might give sinners confidence in a new life of grace; and that of conversion to God he might be an example.[62]

This first biography of Francis seems to fix the moment of conversion in the long illness which struck the saint.

> Worn down by his long illness, as human obstinacy deserves since it is rarely remedied except through punishment, he began to mull over within himself things that were not usual for him. [...] From that day he began to regard himself as worthless and to hold in some contempt what he had previously held as admirable and loveable.[63]

We have however seen that in his Testament, Francis himself places his 'leaving the world' at a different moment, at that moment of meeting with the leper. The expressions he uses leave no doubt about this: 'that which seemed bitter to me was changed into sweetness of soul and body'. The biographer, who certainly knew this passage well, remained unsure of the exact moment of Francis' conversion, partly because he never became a monk and never 'entered religious life' but remained a lay person. In a certain sense one could say that—unlike Anthony and the monks, Francis never left the world because his life continued to unroll in the midst of all the cities, working like everyone else, sleeping in the houses of anyone.

When Francis speaks of 'leaving the world', it is far from certain that he was using the phrase in the technical monastic sense, and there is also another phrase he uses with a far wider spread of meaning: to do penance. This second expression indicates conversion as well, but for Francis it also had a more specifically evangelical significance. In the Gospel of Mark, the first words spoken by Jesus were: 'The time is fulfilled and the Kingdom of God is at hand. Repent—be converted—and believe the Gospel'[64]. In Greek, the word 'converted' is *metanoiete*. Biblical scholars explain that the word means a complete and concrete changing of life, and this is what Jesus asks for with the promised coming of the Kingdom in mind. This conversion of life is asked of everyone, of the Jews too, in fact of the Jews first of all. But for the Christians this *metanoia* means that they, as gentiles, not only change their way of life but also renounce their various pagan religious traditions. In this way the term 'conversion' quickly came to indicate a change of religion as well.

A second difficulty was added in the fourth century when, after the so-called conversion of Constantine, Christianity was first recognised as the legal religion and then as the religion of the Emperor and State. Among many other things, this resulted in infant baptism and finally produced, for the first time, a Christian sociology, that is to say, a large number of Christians who were not Christians by choice but because their parents were Christian or because they lived in a Christian environment. In this context, how were they to understand the gospel invitation to change their way of life? Jerome, the great translator of the Bible into Latin, preferred not to translate *metanoiete* with 'be converted'—a word which existed in classical Latin but with the implication of a change of religion—and instead he used *paenitemini* 'repent' or *paenitentiam agite* 'to do penance'[65]. It was a circumlocution which had the result of explaining that the gospel demanded a profound change in the lives of everyone, including those who were baptised as babies.

'To do penance' then, was the expression used by all Christians, including lay people who wanted to take the Gospel seriously. 'To leave the world' was the expression used by monks who also made external changes in their way of life. When Francis used both expressions at the same time, he introduced a new dimension to the idea of conversion, or perhaps restored an ancient evangelical ideal, that of remaining in the world without being of the world.[66] For this reason Francis never considered his conversion finished. His early biographers show that even when he reached the end of his life, he still repeated: 'Let us begin, brothers, to serve the Lord God, for up until now we have done little or nothing.'[67]

Unlike Thomas of Celano who clearly had difficulties in determining the precise moment of Francis' conversion, Guido of Spoleto and the other ecclesiastics, charged by the pope with gathering evidence about Clare's 'life, conversion, conversation and miracles' had few problems in identifying this moment. In fact the story of the conversion of Clare is entirely focussed around a single episode, one which showed a true and profoundly radical turnaround in her life, namely the moment of her flight from her father's house in order to follow Francis at San Damiano. The *Legend of Saint Clare the Virgin*, which here follows a monastic schema, gives a highly detailed description, rich in information which is not found in the canonisation process and which is the fruit of the personal researches of the author who was well aware of the importance of this theme. Yet what preceded and followed this important gesture of Clare? Also, in Clare's own awareness as much as in that of her fellow citizens, what significance did her conversion assume? In what sense did she change her life?

During the Canonisation Process, the witness who spoke at most length about this was her blood sister, Beatrice, some years her junior. She said that:

> After Saint Francis had heard of the fame of her holiness, he went many times to preach to her, so that the virgin Clare acquiesced to his preaching, renounced the world and all earthly things, and went to serve God as soon as she was able. After that she sold her entire inheritance and part of that of the witness, and gave it to the poor.
>
> Then Saint Francis gave her the tonsure before the altar in the church of the Virgin Mary called the Porziuncola, and then sent her to the church of San Paolo delle Abbadesse. When her relatives wanted to drag her out, Lady Clare grabbed the altar cloths and uncovered her head, showing them she was tonsured. In no way did she acquiesce, neither letting them take her from that place nor remaining with them.[68]

This evidence is used almost to the letter by the Bull of Canonisation:

> After hearing this praise, blessed Francis immediately began to encourage her and to lead her to the perfect service of Christ.
>
> Quickly adhering to the sacred admonitions of this man and desiring to reject entirely the world with everything earthly and to serve the Lord alone in voluntary poverty, she fulfilled this as quickly as she could. At last she finally changed all her goods into alms and distributed them as resources for the poor, so that, one with him, whatever she had she too would consider for the service of Christ.[69]

There are four main elements which emerge from this account of her conversion. The first is her meetings and conversations with Francis. The second is her decision to renounce the world in order to live in poverty and to distribute her goods to the poor. The third is her being given the tonsure by Francis in the little church of the Porziuncola and the fourth is her encounter with her family. The *Legend of Saint Clare the Virgin* takes this ground plan and enriches it with many details, but also makes some important omissions. The account is given three chapters which are entitled: Knowledge and Friendliness with Blessed Francis; How, after she turned from the world through Blessed Francis, she entered Religion; How she faced the assault of her relatives with firm perseverance and came to San Damiano.

The Meeting With Francis

The bull of canonisation, drawing on the evidence of Beatrice, affirms that the initiative for the first meeting between Francis and Clare, was his. The sources, however, do not agree on this point. The biographer prefers to understand that the initiative for their first meeting was of them both or, better, of the Spirit of the Lord, who drew them to each other. It says:

> Hearing of the then celebrated name of Francis, who, like a new man was renewing with new virtues the way of perfection forgotten by the world, she was moved by the Father of the spirits— whose initiatives each one had already accepted, although in different ways—and immediately desired to see and hear him. No less did he desire to see and speak with her, impressed by the widespread fame of so gracious a young lady, so that, in some way, he who was totally longing for spoil and who had come to depopulate the kingdom of the world, would also be able to wrest this noble spoil from the evil world and win her for his Lord.[70]

Another witness in the Canonisation Process maintains, on the other hand, that the initiative certainly belonged to Clare. This is a witness whose evidence must be considered a little more weighty than that of Beatrice who was, at the time of these events, little more than a child. This witness is Bona di Guelfuccio, the personal friend of Clare's youth who said:

> The Lady Clare was always considered by everyone a most pure virgin and has such fervour of spirit she could serve God and please him. Because of this, the witness many times accompanied her to speak to Saint Francis. She went secretly not to be seen by her parents.[71]

The prudence of the biographer in speaking of a reciprocal attraction seems justified. But another detail, again recounted by Bona di Guelfuccio, leads us to think that the very first sign of interest was shown by Clare, given that

> The Lady Clare, while she was still in the world, also gave the witness a certain amount of money as a votive offering and directed her to carry it to those who were working on Saint Mary of the Porziuncola so that they would sustain the flesh.[72]

'Those who were working at Saint Mary of the Porziuncola' must have been Francis and his companions when, at the beginning of their time as simple penitents, they were working at the restoration of the little church down on the plain below Assisi. Clare was already aware of the life of the first companions of Francis because her cousin Rufino had chosen to join them. At that point, she was a young woman intent on works of charity who, as Bona said at the Process, 'had great fervour of spirit with which to serve God and please Him'. In other words, Clare—at this period of her life—was a woman who was searching. Urged to marry, she seemed always to be rejecting the chance to become a good, Christian noble woman like her mother. At the same time, she did not know what path to take instead. The gesture of sending a little money to those working near the Porziuncola was, possibly, an implicit request for help.

The affirmation of the *Legend*, according to which Clare sought to meet Francis moved by 'the Father of Spirits– whose initiatives each one had already accepted, although in different ways' takes on a different colour in the light of the evidence in the Process. Certainly the meeting with Francis was decisive for Clare and all the sources give it a high profile, but at the moment when this meeting happened, she was not an uncertain little girl but a young woman who had lived with her religious and human uncertainties for some while. As the *Legend* says, Clare and Francis were both inspired by the Lord, although in different ways. This meeting with Francis was, for Clare, the decisive event which changed her life, but even before the meeting, she was a young lady who 'sought to please the Lord' and 'freely went to find the poor'. She was a young woman whose holiness was already known among her fellow citizens.

Many years after this incident, in a difficult moment for her religious family, Clare turned to the memory of this and wrote:

> After the most High Heavenly Father saw fit by his grace to enlighten my heart to do penance according to the example and teaching of our most blessed father Saint Francis, shortly after his own conversion, I, together with my sisters, willingly promised him obedience.[73]

The accent falls strongly on 'willingly' (in Latin *voluntarie*): Clare, even across many years, insists that her choice was a free one. At eighteen she was young, but not so very young by the canons of knightly society. Above all she was not naïve or ingenuous, hers was a choice made with full awareness.

The *Legend* also underlines Clare's strength of will when it moves on to speak of the meetings she had with Francis in which

> He visited her and she more frequently him, moderating the times of their visits so that this divine pursuit could not be perceived by anyone nor objected to by gossip. For, with only one close companion accompanying her, the young girl, leaving her paternal home, frequented the clandestine meetings with the man of God, whose words seemed to her to be on fire and whose deeds were seen to be beyond the human.[74]

So it was Clare who most often went to find Francis, not the other way round. Certainly it would have been easier for her to leave her father's house than for him to enter it. But the fact remains that here we see Clare showing a strong spirit of initiative. In fact, Clare's choice presented Francis with a number of problems. The danger of 'public reputation', that is gossip, to which her biographer alludes, was undoubtedly serious. What was most to be feared, however, was not the gossip or the malice—which Francis had often shown did not frighten him—but the family. As Bona di Guelfuccio says: She went secretly, so as not to be seen by her relatives. Francis who personally knew the weight of paternal disapproval, very clearly understood the possible reaction of a family that had already formulated matrimonial plans with Clare at the centre.

Flight From Her Father's House

In any case, the meetings between Francis and Clare could not have gone on for more than a few months. All the sources testify to Clare's urgency to 'leave the world'. As the *Legend* says:

Why dwell on many things? The virgin did not withhold her consent for very long because of the insistent most holy father and his role as a skilful agent of the most faithful Groom.[75]

However, Bona di Guelfuccio, the most important witness of these events was not present at the critical moment. As she herself testifies:

Asked how the Lady Clare was converted, she replied Saint Francis had cut off her hair in the church of Saint Mary of the Porziuncola, as she had heard, because she, the witness, was not present since she had already gone to Rome to observe Lent.

She also said the Lady Clare, before her hair had been cut, had sent her to visit the church of Saint James because the Lady Clare was full of grace and wanted others to be full.[76]

So the biographer had to have recourse to other sources and succeeded each time in putting together an articulate description to what he also realised was the decisive moment in Clare's life. He says:

The solemnity of the Day of Palms was at hand when the young girl went with fervent heart to the man of God, asking him about her conversion and how it should be carried out. The father Francis told her that on the day of the feast she should go, dressed and adorned, together with the crowd of people to receive a palm, and on the following night, leaving the camp she should turn her worldly joy into mourning the Lord's passion.

Therefore when the Sunday came, the young girl, thoroughly radiant with festive splendour among the crowd of women, entered the Church with the others. Then something occurred that was a fitting omen: as the others were going to receive the palms, while Clare remained immobile in her place out of shyness, the Bishop, coming down the steps, came to her and placed a palm in her hands. On that night, preparing to obey the command of the saint, she embarked upon her long desired flight with a virtuous companion. Since she was not content to leave by the usual door, marvelling at her strength, she broke open with her own hands, that other door that is customarily blocked by wood and stone.

And so she ran to Saint Mary of the Porziuncola, leaving behind her home, city and relatives. There the brothers, who were observing sacred vigils before the little altar of God, received the virgin Clare with torches. There, immediately after rejecting the filth of Babylon, she gave the world a bill of divorce. There, her hair shorn by the hands of the brothers, she put aside every kind of fine dress.[77]

There are several observations to be made about this account, above all, that Clare's flight from her father's house was situated in a liturgical context. The detail about Palm Sunday, which is only told in the *Legend*, is particularly interesting. Palm Sunday, in fact, introduces Holy Week and is usually called The First Sunday of the Passion. On that day in the Western Church, before the baptism of children became so widespread, it was usual to baptise the catechumens. The liturgy of this Sunday begins with the festive celebration of Jesus' entry into Jerusalem and then ends with the reading of the Passion.

The whole account seems to recall the structure of the liturgy. Clare, on the instructions of Francis, was to dress herself 'elegantly and adorned' in order to celebrate, with the whole city, the joy of the Lord's entry into Jerusalem, but then, during the night, she was to abandon that joy in order to despoil herself of her fine clothes, and to follow the Lord whom she had seen change His joy at His royal entry into His city, into the sorrow of the way of the cross. All the details had been thought through. The stress of the brothers waiting for Clare with their lamps lit, shows that this source for the biography must have been an eye witness of the event. The one who had prepared this 'liturgical flight' was, as the *Legend* says, Francis himself. It was he, a simple layman, who 'invented' a liturgy in order worthily to welcome Clare in the name of the Lord. It was a liturgy which encompassed the whole span of the day and could only have come from the religious imagination of the saint who later 'invented' the liturgy of the crib at Greccio. In that Christmas scene, too, we are dealing with a true and genuine liturgy which Francis had worked on for two weeks previously. Some of the details, like the night, the lighted lamps, the sense of joy were particularly significant in both episodes.

The heart of this liturgy lies in the moment when Clare, leaving her home and coming out of the city, arrives at Saint Mary of the Angels. There, setting aside her aristocratic clothing, she is clothed with the garment of the poor who lived on the plain around Assisi and she allowed her hair to be cut by Francis. This was certainly an unusual gesture, so much so that the *Legend* prefers to use a more general phrase, saying that 'her hair was cut by the brothers'. The witness given at the Canonisation Process and indeed the Bull *Clara claris praeclara* leave us in no doubt: Clare's hair was cut before the altar of the Porziuncola by Francis himself.

In recent times, many authors have reflected on the significance of this tonsure. Paul Sabatier, in his famous *Vie de saint Francois d'Assisi* sees it as a moment of great ecclesiastical freedom on the part of the saint who, according to Sabatier:

> was too much of an idealist to be prudent or to conform to any pretentious custom of good manners. As for the foundation of the Order of Brothers, he sought counsel from nobody but himself and God. This was his strength: if he had hesitated or even if he

had simply submitted himself to ecclesiastical rules, he would have been brought to a halt twenty times over before he could have achieved anything. The hagiographic sources seem to ignore the strength of this argument that Francis was ignorant of canonical rules. He, a simple deacon, arrogated to himself the right to receive the vows of Clare and to give her the tonsure without any novitiate.[78]

The accuracy of this judgement is partly undermined by the image of what the sisters became after the death of Clare. In order to understand the force of this tonsure which Francis gave her, we need to pose a simple question: after this liturgy, what had Clare become? Was she a professed nun in spite of having made no novitiate, as Sabatier underlines? The answer to this question is: certainly not! Clare promised to observe no rule, she did not receive a monastic veil, she did not enter any settled, canonically erected community. As Luigi Padovese has definitively shown[79], the tonsure before the altar of Saint Mary of the Porziuncola was not a monastic consecration but a penitential gesture. Clare did not become a nun but a penitent, a *mulier religiosa*, a religious woman, a woman of penance. As the *Legend* says, through this liturgy she received the 'insignia of penance'. At that moment, Francis and his companions too were only penitents, men of penance. They welcomed Clare as one of themselves.

The problem then became: what to do with a woman in such a fraternity? Many years later when the problem had significantly grown numerically, the brothers themselves made a decision about those women who asked to share their life of penance. This decision is reflected in the Regola non Bullata where it says:

> Absolutely no woman may be received to obedience by any brother, but after spiritual advice has been given to her, let her do penance wherever she wants.[80]

So what did Clare do then? According to the *Legend*, Francis and his companions behaved towards her exactly as set out in the Regola non Bullata:

> After she received the insignia of holy penance before the altar of the blessed Virgin and, as if before the throne of this Virgin, the humble servant was married to Christ, Saint Francis immediately led her to the church of San Paolo to remain there until the Most High would provide another place.[81]

Conflict With Her Family

The Bull of Canonisation mentioned above, had underlined how, at San Paolo delle Abbadesse

> When her relations endeavoured to bring her back, she immediately took hold of the altar and its cloths, and resisted her relatives strongly and firmly in this way. She could not permit herself to be separated from God's service because she was already joined to Him with her whole mind.[82]

The *Legend* is more precise:

> But after the news reached her relatives, they condemned with a broken heart the deed and proposal of the virgin and, banding together as one, they ran to the place attempting to obtain what they could not. They employed violent force, poisonous advice and flattering promises, persuading her to give up such a worthless deed that was unbecoming to her class and without precedent in her family. But taking hold of the altar cloths, she bared her tonsured head, maintaining that she would in no way be torn away from the service of Christ. With the increasing violence of her relatives, her spirit grew and her love, provoked by injuries, provided strength. So for many days, even though she endured an obstacle

in the way of the Lord and her own relatives opposed her proposal of holiness, her spirit did not crumble and her fervour did not diminish. Instead, amid word and seeds of hatred, she moulded her spirit anew in hope until her relatives, turning back, were quiet.[83]

San Paolo delle Abbadesse was an important Benedictine abbey on the slopes of Monte Subasio. It was therefore well known. To join somewhere with a monastic context would certainly not have seemed an unsuitable choice for a young aristocratic girl. Why then did her relatives, according to the *Legend* see Clare's choice as 'a kind of ignoble condition which was unworthy of the dignity of the family and which had no precedent in the city'? In Latin the text reads: '*suadentes ab huiusmodi vilitate discedere*' which translated literally means: 'persuading her to withdraw from the servility of such a deed'. The term *vilitas* in classical Latin means that which is of little value, of small importance and therefore 'low or vulgar' while in medieval Latin it came to indicate the condition of those who were not noble and did not behave as such. A nobleman who behaved with *vilitas* was one who had committed some sort of crime, who had not kept faith with his word, or who had betrayed his origins.

Clare, then, was guilty of *vilitas*, of betraying her proper condition as an aristocrat. Her relatives wanted to distance themselves from this *vilitas*. All this only makes sense in the light of one simple explanation: Clare had not entered San Paolo delle Abbadesse as a nun but as a servant, as a *conversa*. This would be the perfect status for a penitent. There is no other explanation. To be welcomed as a nun in an important monastery like San Paolo, it was necessary to come with a dowry. This was a custom which the Fourth Lateran Council tried to remedy a few years later, but at the time when Clare made her choice, it was widely practised.

When Clare presented herself at the doors of San Paolo delle

Abbadesse, she no longer had any goods to offer as a dowry because she had sold them. According to the order of events identified in the Bull of Canonisation, Clare

> Changed all her goods into alms and distributed them as resources for the poor, so that one with him, whatever she had she too would consider for the service of Christ. Then, fleeing from the clamour of the world, she went down to the church in the field and, after receiving the sacred tonsure from blessed Francis himself, she proceeded to another.[84]

What were the goods in question? The evidence of Clare's sister Beatrice is more detailed:

> She sold her entire inheritance and part of that of the witness and gave it to the poor.[85]

The word *inheritance* is more than likely to mean the dowry. Among central Italian aristocratic families at around the first half of the thirteenth century, we see a transition from the bride gift (an ancient Germanic tradition in which the husband would give the wife a notable portion of their patrimony) to that of a dowry (in which the father of the bride provides for her future needs). In practice this transition meant that the bride's family themselves held the control of this transaction. At the same time the hereditary practice was changing: the daughter did not receive her share of the father's goods at his death but on her marriage, at the moment which maximised the advantages to the family who thereby ensured a favourable alliance with another group of families.

It is likely that Clare, following the custom of the time, had received her dowry before she left her house and home. In fact, the accent on the inheritance of the sister, Beatrice, who was much younger, suggests that this inheritance had been given to them in childhood, most likely we are here speaking about movable goods such a jewels and valuable clothes, which did not encroach on the immovable patrimony and inheritance of the family which, presumably, would have been destined for the male heirs. Clare did not use her inheritance to obtain a good marriage that would have served to strengthen the system of alliances around her family. Instead she sold these goods and distributed the proceeds to the poor. Then she presented herself, poor, at the door of San Paolo delle Abbadesse, to be accepted as a servant. This was the *vilitas* which so enraged her relatives.

Examined in this light, the story of Clare's conversion looks much more like that of Francis' than at first appeared. He too had to deal with the hostility of his own family. Arnaldo Fortini suggests that Clare had first heard of Francis through the urchins in the street shouting at the son of Bernadone when he appeared in beggar's rags for the first time. In another monastery on the road to Gubbio, Francis had reassumed the condition of a servant or 'oblate'—at that time almost the same—which he had had when he was the servant of the priest at San Damiano. This same condition, this same status, seems to have been Clare's when she came to San Paolo delle Abbadesse.

Clare's response to her relatives' threats also deserves a comment. She, it seems, grasped the altar cloth and uncovered her head, showing the sign of the tonsure. At this point her relatives dared no longer touch her which shows that the tonsure indicated to them that Clare was already 'vowed' to the Lord and therefore outside their jurisdiction. The Church did, in fact, recognise the status of the devout woman or devout religious (*mulier devota* or *religiosa*) as not only meaning the professed nun but also women who had begun a life of penance even while remaining in their own homes. Francis, too, had enjoyed exactly the same protection.

This realisation casts light on the significance of the gesture before the altar of Saint Mary of the Porziuncola. If we cannot call this a monastic consecration, we are all the same speaking of a decisive moment in the life of Clare, when she renounced all in order to follow the Lord, and the author of the *legend* was well aware of this. This renunciation and this choice took place in the hands of Francis. Let us not forget that Francis at this time was twenty-six and Clare eighteen. The responsibility of the young penitent is clear, but what is also clear is the trust with which the young aristocratic girl confided herself to this man whom many considered a madman.

Clare's choice, following the advice of Francis, was an entirely spiritual one. The moment of decision on that Palm Sunday, from which all the rest flowed, is one of maximum interest. From then on, Clare set herself as a poor woman to follow the poor Christ on the road of the Cross. Her renunciation of her wealthy clothes, her self-despoiling as her passage to the following of Christ who had nothing but the Cross, all had a powerful spiritual significance.

This profoundly spiritual choice had at the same time, however, some deeply human consequences, both personal and social. Clare left her home and with that also left the family's projected plans in her regard. She definitively renounced the option for marriage. Above all she, the noblewoman, assumed the condition of a servant. Hers was indeed a change of heart but also a change of status. The reactions released in the heart of the family by such a choice are easily understandable, but we gain an even deeper insight into Clare from another major witness at the Process. Sr Cristiana de Messer Bernardo said:

… in selling her inheritance, Lady Clare's relatives wanted her to give them a better price. She did not want to sell it to them but sold it to others so the poor would not be defrauded. All she received from the sale of the inheritance, she distributed to the poor.[86]

The expressions which she uses come from the heart of the Franciscan tradition. Even Francis, at least according to his companions, often said, 'I was never a robber: by that I mean that for the alms which are the inheritance of the poor, I have always accepted less than I needed so that I would not defraud the other poor. To act otherwise would be to steal'[87] meaning that he had never been a thief. The thought is extremely simple: God created good things for the benefit of everyone; if someone has a large amount of good things, they are a gift until we meet someone who is more needy than we are who may then claim the portion which they lack. The sources are full of incidents, such as that of the woman with the eye illness who could not pay the doctor:

> Blessed Francis, moved with compassion, immediately called one of his companions who was his guardian and said to him: Brother Guardian, we must return our neighbour's property. What neighbour's property, Brother? The mantle we received as a loan from that poor woman, we must give it back to her.[88]

When Clare sold her inheritance and distributed it to the poor, she was not so much making a gesture of charity as a gesture of justice. For her it was a question of the restitution of legitimate property. Therefore, it would have been pointless to sell it to her relatives, even if they offered her a far better price, for she would have been deepening the robbery which the rich had already made of the goods of the poor. Clare, like Francis, had no wish to be a thief.

· · · · ·

PENITENCE

The liturgy which took place at Saint Mary of the Angels in the Porziuncola did not introduce Clare to the monastic life but, more simply, to the life of penitence. At San Paolo delle Abbadesse her condition was that of a penitent in the service of the choir nuns. Status as a penitent was usually guaranteed by the Church which offered special protection and, in effect, considered the penitent an ecclesiastical person and exempt therefore from civil jurisdiction.

Some days after the encounter with her parents, Clare left San Paolo and sought refuge in the church of Sant'Angelo in Panzo.[89] What was the thinking behind this decision? It has been suggested that Clare was seeking a safer haven from her family's reaction, or that the nuns of Monte Subasio were fearful at the possibility of a return visit from this powerful family and had wanted her to leave their monastery. In any case, Clare chose to settle not near another monastery but in a community of women living near a church. The fact that the Bull of Canonisation does not refer at this point to an established religious community, and also the fact that the women at Sant'Angelo in Panzo were drawn into the Damianite orbit, suggests that this community had from the beginning been a group of those *mulieres religiosae*, those

numerous religious woman, who had chosen to live an evangelical life
together without adopting any approved rule.

In Central Italy of the first half of the thirteenth century, and especially in Umbria, this phenomenon had assumed considerable pro-
portions. These groups of women who wanted to live a life of prayer
and penitence together, did not necessarily find what they sought in
the traditional monastic channels. An analogous development has
been noted in other regions of Europe at that time, above all in
Brabant and around the Rhine where the same flowering of prayer
experiences, of charity and the life of penitence led to the development of the great Beguinages of northern Europe.

At Sant'Angelo in Panzo, Clare was joined by her sister Agnes.[90]
The account of this second young girl's flight from the house of
Favarone di Offreduccio is only given in the *Legend* while the process
is silent about it. The extreme detail and the precision of the account
leads one to think that the author had been able to hear it from the
lips of Agnes herself. Clare then, according to the *Legend*:

> had a sister, tender in age, a sister by flesh and by purity. In her
> desire for her conversion, among the first prayers that she offered
> to God with all her heart, she more ardently begged this grace
> that, just as she had an affinity of spirit with her sister in the world,
> she might also have now a unity of will in the service of God.[91]

So Clare did not want to be alone. At the least, she wanted her sister
to join her. According to the *Legend,* Agnes's desire to follow Clare
was no less:

> A marvellous mutual love had taken hold of both of them, a love
> that, to both, brought a new division, a sorrowful division although
> with feelings diverse.[92]

So,

> Sixteen days after the conversion of Clare, Agnes, inspired by the
> divine spirit, ran to her sister, revealed the secret of her will and
> told her that she wished to serve God completely. Embracing her
> with joy, Clare said: I thank God, most sweet sister, that He has
> heard my concern for you.[93]

There were two problems: the first was that Agnes was only sixteen
and therefore a good bit younger than her sister; the second was that,
unlike Clare, she had not received the tonsure and therefore did not
enjoy the protection of the Church. Therefore, as we see in the
account of the *Legend*:

> While the joyous sisters were clinging to the footprints of Christ
> in the church of Sant'Angelo in Panzo, and she who had heard
> more from the Lord was teaching her novice sister, new attacks by
> relatives were quickly flaring up against the young girls. The next
> day, hearing that Agnes had gone off to Clare, twelve men, burn-
> ing with anger and hiding outwardly their evil intent, ran to the
> place and pretended to make a peaceful entrance. Immediately
> they turned to Agnes, since they had long ago lost hope of Clare,
> and said: Why have you come to this place? Get ready immediately
> to return with us.[94]

The relatives were trying to do with Agnes what the tonsure had pre-
vented them doing with Clare: seizing her and forcing her to go back
with them Here, according to the testimony of the *Legend*, divine
power intervened and, in answer to Clare's entreaty, made Agnes's
body so heavy that all those men were unable to lift it up. At this
Uncle Monaldo who was the leader of that armed force, tried to
strike her hard, but a sudden pain seized his arm. This was how Clare

was able, single-handed, to overcome all those who opposed her sister's choice.

Only when the deed was done did Francis appear. The *Legend* continues:

> After they departed with a bitter spirit at their unfinished business, Agnes got up joyfully and, already rejoicing in the cross of Christ for which she had struggled in this first battle, gave herself perpetually to the divine service. In fact, Blessed Francis cut off her hair with his own hand and directed her, together with her sister, in the way of the Lord.[95]

The arrival of Agnes radically altered Clare's situation, for now she was no longer alone. It was no longer a question of finding a suitable place for her to live her life of penance, but one of bringing to birth a new female community of evangelical life. At this point, Francis thought of a more suitable place for Clare, Agnes and the others who were going to join them, and that was the church of San Damiano where he himself had begun to live a life according to the Gospel. Again it is the *Legend* which tells us that at the advice of Francis she moved to San Damiano.[96]

In this journey which led Clare to San Damiano, some have seen a kind of passage through the different experiences of women's religious life of the time, from Benedictine monasticism at San Paolo delle Abbadesse to the *mulieres religiosae* of Sant'Angelo in Panzo. In reality, however, as we have seen, Clare understood herself to be simply a penitent in all these situations. It was only at this later point that she began to consider giving life to a new form of community.

Soon Clare and Agnes were joined by Pacifica, the sister of Bona, and then by Benvenuta from a noble family, of Perugia, and slowly by others. They were a lovely group of young women, mostly of aristocratic origin, whose juridical situation was far from clear. Certainly Bishop Guido, on whom the little church of San Damiano depended, knew about them and approved. On the other hand, as the *Legend* expressly says with regard to Agnes, the sisters were directed by young lay penitent, namely Francis, who had no canonical authority for such a responsibility. Also they did not live under any approved rule.

Clare and her companions, by affiliating or (better) incorporating themselves into the Franciscan Fraternity, embraced the life of penance which characterised that of Francis.[97]

There is a passage in the Rule of Clare in which we seem to catch a glimpse of her thoughts about these early moments in the San Damiano community:

> After the Most High heavenly Father saw fit by His grace to enlighten my heart to do penance according to the example and teaching of our most blessed father Saint Francis, shortly after his own conversion, I, together with my sisters, willingly promised him obedience. When the Blessed Father saw we had no fear of poverty, hard work, trial, shame or contempt of the world, but instead we held them as great delights, moved by piety he wrote a form of life for us as follows:
>
> Because by divine inspiration you have made yourselves daughters and handmaids of the most High, most Exalted King, the heavenly Father, and have taken the Holy Spirit as your spouse, choosing to live according to the perfection of the holy Gospel, I resolve and promise for myself and for my brothers, always to have the same loving care and special solicitude for you as for them. As long as he lived, he diligently fulfilled this and wished that it always be fulfilled by the brothers.[98]

The importance of this passage can be measured by the fact that in it, Clare openly contradicts the Regula non Bullata of Francis which, as we have seen, forbids receiving women to obedience. It says:

> Absolutely no woman may be received to obedience by any brother, but after spiritual advice has been given to her, let her do penance wherever she wants.[99]

Evidently Clare wanted here, in a official document like the Rule, to stress that Francis had chosen to make an exception for her and her companions and that he had received them to obedience.

The expression that Clare uses to describe her new way of life is the same as that used by Francis in his Testament: to do penance:

> After the Most High heavenly Father saw fit by His grace to enlighten my heart to do penance according to the example and teaching of our most blessed father Saint Francis ...[100]

Clare and the other sisters were women of penance, but what did this really mean in the realities of thirteenth-century life? Penance was a definite state,

> An attitude before life and death, a way of confronting oneself and others, an attitude which encompassed the whole world, people and God in a 'state' an existential situation.[101]

Within this understanding, penance for men and women of the thirteenth century not only meant a religious dimension but a cultural condition in the fullest sense. For Francis this became the fundamental human condition. For him to be a man meant to be a man of penance because a relationship with God is implicit in our being human. From this it follows that to be in relationship with God means to be less, to be humble, a sinner, a penitent. Penance is the condition of one who knows God, the only condition possible for us before God, the only condition possible for us who, drawn by Christ, seek to insert ourselves into love.

The earliest source for the Franciscan movement is in a famous letter written by a bishop from across the Alps, Jacques de Vitry. He had gone down into Italy in 1216, to the pontifical court, in order to receive his episcopate and then to travel on to the Middle East. From Genoa, he wrote back to his friends in Belgium. Even though some four years had elapsed since the start of the San Damiano experiment, the letter is extremely interesting about this feminine branch of the Franciscan family which is here shown in sharp relief:

> I found one consolation in these parts, nevertheless: many men and women, rich and worldly, after renouncing everything for Christ, fled the world. They are called Lesser Brothers and Lesser Sisters. They are held in great esteem by the Lord Pope and the cardinals. They do not occupy themselves with temporal affairs, but work each day with great desire and enthusiastic zeal to capture those souls that were perishing from the vanities of the world and employing themselves in contemplation. The women live near the cities in various hospices. They accept nothing but live from the work of their hands. In fact, they are very much offended and disturbed because they are honoured by the clergy and laity more than they deserve.[102]
>
> I really believe that before the end of the world, the Lord wants to save many souls through these simple and poor men and to put the prelates to shame for they have become like silent watchdogs, unable to bark.[103]

Jacques de Vitry arrived in Perugia where he joined up with the papal court, just a few days after the death of Innocent III. Jacques brought with him the request of some 'pious women' whom he had known and visited in the diocese of Liège. These women were not, at that time, well known in France and Germany, as he himself wrote:

> I sought permission for these religious women to be able to live together in community houses, not only in the diocese of Liège but also in the whole Empire, and to encourage each other by sharing the fruits of their good works.[104]

Jacques himself had written the official *Legend* of one of them, Mary of Oignies, with the intention of promoting her canonisation.

So this bishop who has left us the first external account of the Franciscan movement, was a man with his finger on the pulse of almost the whole religious ferment in Europe at that time. As Herbert Grundmann has written:

> Jacques de Vitry had come to the Curia as representative of this women's religious movement in Belgium, Northern France and Germany, and he was probably the first to see and recognise the full complexity, the common characteristics and underlying significance of the women's religious movements in different European countries at the beginning of the 13th century. As a Canon Regular of St Augustine, he had lived for some years as protector, confessor and promoter of Mary of Oignies. She was the heart of the women's religious movement in Belgium and had, at one time, intended to go among the Albigensians in southern France 'to give honour to God in the place where He had been abandoned by so many'. After her death on 23 June 1213, Jacques had written her biography in order to confront the French heretics with the image of a 'modern saint'. When Jacques then travelled into Italy to meet the curia, he found before his eyes exactly the same situation, namely, that the Humiliati in Lombardy and the Franciscans in

Umbria were both, like the Belgian religious, living out the ideals of poverty and chastity. Even though they were sometimes tinged with heresy, yet they were, to his mind, the representatives in the Church of the only energy capable of overcoming on the one hand, the heresy, and on the other hand the decadence and torpor of ecclesiastical life.[105]

In all these movements, there was plenty of room for women. This is a phenomenon which Raol Manselli has highlighted:

> Something which characterised this popular religion of the early Middle Ages was the fervent and active part played by women. [...] After the turn of the century, women are seen to be participants in religious life in new and very varied ways. They took part in the Crusades, they followed itinerant preachers, they had visions and revelations, they participated according to their own particular insights into the spiritual life, as did the two women Agnes and Clare of Assisi.[106]

Why were women so especially attracted to this new religious movement. What were its characteristics? The same Jacques de Vitry speaks about it in this way:

> Certain devout and prudent virgins, not wishing to live in their father's house amid people who were worldly and not chaste and therefore in great and grave danger, particularly these days, took refuge instead in monasteries which the Lord had multiplied throughout the world. Those who were not able to enter monasteries, chose to gather together and live in a house [...] under the discipline of one who was their superior in integrity and prudence. She would instruct them in letters if that were the custom, and through vigils, prayer, fasting and other afflictions, through manual labour and poverty, abjection and humility.[107]

These women, then were not nuns because they did not live in monasteries but in private houses. There they lived a sort of religious life, marked by prayer, manual work, poverty and exercises of penance. This last aspect is the one which most strikes anybody who reads the hagiographic sources of this period. The practice of fasting and other afflictions—to use Jacques de Vitry's expression—seems extremely severe, especially for women, so much so that some scholars have seen it as almost a pathological symptom.[108] In many ways San Damiano did not differ much from these communities of women who lived a religious life' in chaste penance'. Even Clare's prayer, fasting and other penances were not very different from those of many other religious women of the time.

It is very interesting, therefore, to note that it was precisely concerning the practice of penance that we have a record of dissension between Clare and Francis.[109] This episode refers to the problem of fasting. During those first years at San Damiano, Clare not only fasted twice a week in ordinary time and every day during Lent, as was the monastic custom. In addition she alternated these fast days with days on which she did not eat at all. The biographer does not hide his amazement:

> So that you who hear these things might marvel at what you cannot imitate, she took nothing in the way of food on three days of the week during those Lents, that is, on Monday, Wednesday and Friday. Thus after one another, the days of a meagre meal and those of strict mortification followed one another so that a vigil of perfect fast passed over into a quasi-feast of bread and water. It is not surprising that such rigour, observed for a long period of time, subjected Clare to sicknesses, consumed her strength and enervated the vigour of her body.[110]

Faced with the fact that Clare was becoming sick, Francis and the Bishop of Assisi forbad this fast of three days and commanded her not to let a day pass without eating at least an ounce and a half of bread by way of food. The stress on the intervention of Bishop Guido is interesting, partly because it shows that San Damiano was a community of religious women who were subject to the ordinary of the diocese, just as the little church of San Damiano depended directly on the bishop. Above all, though, it is interesting because it shows that Clare put up a certain resistance to Francis when he tried to mitigate her fasting. It reveals that Francis and Clare had different ideas about penance. Clare would not have dared oppose the one to whom, in her own words, she had promised obedience, had she not felt it to be something decisive for her religious identity.

This divergence about penance is also found in the matter of beds or, better, the place where Clare slept. The *Legend* says:

> The bare ground and sometimes branches of vines were her bed and a hard piece of wood under her head took the place of a pillow. But in the course of time when her body became weak, she placed a mat on the ground and indulged her head with a little bit of straw. After a long illness began to take hold of her weakened body and the blessed Francis had commanded it, she used a sack filled with straw.[111]

The detail about vine branches is interesting: Clare did not limit herself to sleeping on the bare ground (as many penitents had done including Francis himself) but she added further suffering. In this sense again her concept of penance was different than Francis'. He was indeed a man of penance in the full meaning of the word because he lived out a total despising of himself and his own body, finally arriving at a degree of self-neglect that—unless his guardian insisted—he did not sleep or slept very little and ate little or nothing. Externally then, the practices of the two did not much differ but Francis never sought useless suffering, penance for him did not include harming himself but only a distancing from himself. The difference might seem subtle but it is decisive. In the *Legend of Perugia* there is a passage (which reappears in the Fioretti) concerning the so-called Chapter of Mats, in which it says:

> The first brothers and for a long time those who came after them mortified their bodies not only by excessive abstinence from drink and food but even by vigils, the cold and manual work. They even wore cinctures made of iron and cuirasses if they could obtain them and also the roughest hair-shirts they could find. That is why the saintly Father, considering that the brothers could become sick from this practice—which is what did happen in a short time to many of them—forbade, in a chapter, any brother from wearing anything on his flesh except his tunic.
>
> We who lived with him can testify to this about him: from the time he had brothers and throughout all his life, he practiced the virtue of discretion for them (keeping always intact our Order's required poverty and virtue, which are traditional among the senior brothers).[112]

Clare shared the excessive penitential ardour of Francis' first companions. Perhaps what we have here is not so much just a more or less bland application of penance, but two different ideas about penance itself.

In those years when the minorite fraternity was beginning, there was—throughout central Italy—a certain spirit of dualism of which one variant is the Cathar heresy. The teaching of this group proposed a fundamental spiritual dualism: good and evil. For the Cathars, the spirit had been created by the god of good while the flesh had been created by the god of evil. In their cosmology and their dealings with individuals, these groups made this distinction between the god of good and the god of evil. All of them, however, applied a rigorous morality sustained by a strong rejection of everything connected with the flesh. Some went so far as to undergo the 'Endurance' which was a purification rite that could end in death. This religious suicide was seen by the Cathars as the equivalent of martyrdom and those who practised it were held in veneration as having attained the heights of perfection. This is why, in modern times, the Cathar heresy has been called the 'heresy of evil'. It cannot be denied that some currents of penitential thinking ran parallel with the Catharist concept of perfection as an asceticism competition, and mortification was seen as proof of holiness. In this competition, women took the lead precisely because the prejudices of the time held that women are 'naturally' prone to sin (as the dedicatory letter to the *Legend* notes). Religious women had, in a sense, to prove even more than their masculine brothers that they knew how to overcome the sinful limitations of their flesh.

Francis' attitude to the heretics of his time was not that of doctrinal or theological condemnation so much as one of taking a distance existentially. For him the sensible world was not evil; on the contrary it was good because it had been created by God who is good. This is the experience behind the *Canticle of Creation*, which can also be seen as a joyous and strong refutation of every dualistic and pessimistic idea about creation. For this reason Francis looked at his body with detachment but not with hostility. For him, this was 'Brother Ass' who needed to be kept in control but also thanked for the services he rendered.[113] In this context, the famous episode of the cauterisation which the saint underwent to heal his eyes, is indicative:

At the time of an eye disease, he is forced to let himself be treated.
A surgeon is called to the place and when he comes he is carrying an iron instrument for cauterising. He ordered it to be placed in the fire until it became red hot. But the blessed Father, to comfort the body which was struck with panic, spoke to the fire: My Brother Fire, your beauty is the envy of all creatures, the Most High created you strong, beautiful and useful. Be gracious to me in this hour, be courteous! For a long time I have loved you in the Lord. I pray the great Lord who created you to temper now your heat so that I may bear your gentle burning.[114]

So we see that Francis did not despise his own body when it was filled with fear, but rather comforted it, praying to the Lord.

The reason for the misunderstanding between Francis and Clare about the practices of penance must therefore have arisen through the disciple's difficulty in understanding what exactly Francis meant by penance. Exteriorly, he seemed to be excessively severe towards his own body, but in reality this severity was not generated by a punitive intention but by the distance he had placed between himself and the needs and satisfactions of the flesh. With time Clare seemed to grasp this lesson. Thus in the Third Letter to Agnes of Prague she recalls Francis who advised and directed us to show every possible discretion in matters of food[115] for the weak and the sick. In the Rule too:

the sisters may have little mantles for convenience and propriety in serving and working. In fact let the abbess, with discernment, provide them with clothing according to the diversity of persons, places, seasons and cold climates as in necessity she shall deem expedient.[116]

In the last years of her life, Clare had to undergo the test of a long illness. She learned about suffering through this but, thanks to the example of Francis, she knew not to fear it. The true penance of Clare's last years was not so much the suffering itself, as the acceptance of all suffering in a spirit of praise. Here, in a certain sense, the disciple not only followed the master but took the vision of the master even further. This is because Clare at San Damiano was surrounded by sisters with whom she shared everything, even difficult and testing times. It is as if in those last years of her life, the body of Clare was extended to include all the sisters as well. The whole community of San Damiano became an extended body in which Clare was sensitive to suffering and waiting. As Sr Filippa di Leonardo di Gislerio said at the canonisation process:

> The witness also said that when one of the sisters, Sister Andrea da Ferrara, was suffering from a scrofula in her throat, Lady Clare knew by inspiration she was very tempted by her desires for a cure. One night, while Sister Andrea was below in the dormitory, she squeezed her throat with her own hands so strongly she lost her voice. The holy mother knew this through the Spirit. Then she immediately called the witness who slept near her and told her: Go down immediately to the dormitory because Sister Andrea is seriously ill; boil an egg and give it to her to swallow. After she has recovered her speech, bring her to me'. And so it was done. When the Lady asked Sister Andrea what had been the matter, Sister Andrea did not want to tell her. Then the attentive Lady told her everything in detail as it had happened. And this spread about among the sisters.[117]

If, for Francis, true penance was the full acceptance of every suffering which came to his body, for Clare true penance became, little by little, the full acceptance of every suffering which came to any member of her extended body, that is, of the whole community.

• • • • • •

CHAPTER
SIX

CLARE AND THE
PAPACY

The Bull of Canonisation strongly
underlines that Clare

was, above all, a lover and firm supporter of poverty. She so rooted
it in her spirit, so fixed it in her desires that, firmer in love of it and
more ardent in its embrace, she never departed from her stronger
and delightful union with it for any necessity.[118]

The author of the *Legend* then takes up the theme and develops it:

The pact that she had established with holy poverty was so great
and brought such love, that she wanted to have nothing but Christ
the Lord and would not permit her sisters to possess anything. In
fact, she considered that the most precious pearl of heavenly desire
which she purchased by selling everything, could not be possessed
with the gnawing concern for temporal things. Through frequent
talks she instilled in her sisters that their dwelling place would be
acceptable to God only when it was rich in poverty and that it
would continue to be secure only if it were always fortified by the
strong watch-tower of the most exalted poverty. She encouraged
them in their little nest of poverty to be conformed to the poor

Christ, whom a poor Mother placed as an infant in a narrow crib. With this special reminder, as if with a jewel of gold, she adorned her breast, so that no speck of the dust of earthly things would enter her.[119]

So from the beginning the experience of Clare who had sold her inheritance and distributed the proceeds to the poor, became in substance a shared experience as well as a model and example for all the sisters. The option for poverty was certainly at the heart of the San Damiano experience and a central preoccupation of Clare's. This emerges clearly from her writings.

Why was poverty so important to Clare? We are never going to understand this if we do not first consider the actual poverty in Italian cities at the beginning of the thirteenth century. The rebirth of the city had profoundly changed the face of poverty in medieval society. During the high Middle Ages, in a rural society characterised by a general penury, the poor were essentially individual cases towards whom others could exercise their Christian charity. In the cities, however, the poor were numerous and visible. They represented a reality which challenged urban society as a whole, as well as the individual. As Michel Mollat has observed:

> The stagnant and individual misery of the country was replaced by the collective misery of the city. The rural poor were generally despised individuals but familiar ones, known and helped by their own people. The urban poor were an anonymous entity, often vagabonds with no other refuge than the community of the marginalised where they shared among themselves.[120]

This new kind of poverty confronted even the Church with a new kind of problem. The various religious groups which sought a return to the simple text of the Gospel, also made the heart of their religious intent an option for voluntary poverty. 'Naked to follow the naked Christ' became almost a slogan for many of the new spiritual currents. At the same time, poverty became a yardstick for judging the apostolic work of the Church itself, as emerges, for example, from the words of the heretic Cathar known as Everino di Steinfeld, in a letter he wrote to St Bernard, saying:

> We alone are the true followers of Christ and the Apostles, because we do not only preach their words but we put them into practice, while you Catholics have completely forgotten them,

And he added, by way of clarification and speaking of monks and canons:

> Those among you who are the more perfect, such as monks and canons regular, even while they do not have personal property but only goods in common, all the same, they do possess these goods.[121]

The monastic and feudal Church struggled for a long time to understand this dispute about poverty. In this context, there is an incident which happened to the same St Bernard, which is very significant. One day,

> At Verfeuil, while St Bernard was preaching, an heretic ironically pointed out how fat and well-fed was the mule he had been riding. And he was not silenced when a monk took the capuche of the saint and showed him how thin the saint's neck was and emaciated by fasting.

> Confronted by the mass of poor people, the monk's personal poverty was not enough for he practised it as an ascetical exercise and a mortification. In the eyes of the mass of poor people living in the city, there was more credibility in the community whose

poverty was not only personal but also communal. This was certainly the meaning of the choice made by Francis and his first companions Above all, it was one of the aspects of Francis' experience which struck Clare herself most forcibly, if it be true that Francis is referred to in the episode when she, still in her father's house, sent alms for the poor men who were working on the church of S Maria della Porziuncola. This gap between a personal poverty seen as an exercise in mortification, and a communal poverty, seen as a freely chosen condition of life without guarantees, is probably at the root of Clare's decision to abandon S Paolo delle Abbadesse.

What did a choice for communal poverty mean at San Damiano? Francis and his companions lived a life without guarantees in an objective poverty: they slept, at least in the early days, in a barn for straw near St Mary of the Angels, or in hospices and leper houses in other cities, sharing the condition of the most marginalised. As the Regola non bollata prescribes:

They must rejoice when they live among people considered of little value and looked down upon, among the poor and powerless, the sick and the lepers, and the beggars by the wayside.[122]

This option was not open to Clare and her companions who were precluded from living that kind of itinerant life. They lived at San Damiano. Certainly this was nothing more than a little church with a dormitory above it. Presently a refectory was built and a few other places and then a wall which defined the community's space. For Clare it was essential that this space remained within the limits of one of the modest buildings of the poor without being transformed into a monastery like San Paolo delle Abbadesse. Clare's commitment to maintaining this ideal of poverty right to the end of her life, emerges clearly from her own Rule. In fact, right at the heart of this text, in

a unique moment when she distances herself from the legislative
texts which were her model, Clare inserts some words which sound
strongly autobiographical.

> When the blessed Father saw that we had no fear of poverty, hard
> work, trial, shame or contempt of the world, but instead held them
> as great delights, moved by piety he wrote a form of life for us.

And a little later she adds:

> As I, together with my sisters, have ever been solicitous to safe-
> guard the holy poverty which we have promised the Lord God
> and blessed Francis, so too the abbesses who shall succeed me in
> office and all the sisters are bound inviolably to observe it to the
> end, that is by not receiving or having possessions or ownership
> either of themselves or through an intermediary, or even anything
> that might reasonably be called ownership, except as much land as
> necessity requires for the integrity and proper seclusion of the
> monastery, and this land may not be cultivated except as a garden
> for the needs of the sisters.[123]

These words seem to touch on the fact that even Francis himself had,
at first, been dubious about whether young women like Clare would
be able to live according to the option for most high poverty as he
and his brothers had done. Clare would have won the 'form of life'
from him, that is the text in which Francis committed himself always
to have special care for them, precisely because they had shown their
devotion to poverty.

Clare's text, apparently so simple, really rested on long years of
reflection and struggle. There is the fact that normally poverty was
associated with contempt. Clare's relatives knew this very well when
they wanted her—at all costs—to abandon her situation as a servant

at San Paolo delle Abbadesse, a situation which was humiliating for the daughter of a noble house. However, Clare had walked in the footprints of Francis and understood that poverty is rather like a beautiful woman who is despised by everyone. This is the theme of the Song of Songs which presents the Bride as 'black but beautiful'. It is also the theme of a composition which has generated a great deal of discussion among specialists and which is much loved by those who seek God: the *Sacrum Commercium sancti Francisci cum Domina Paupertate* or the Sacred Exchange of Saint Francis and Lady Poverty. We cannot say for certain that Clare had been able to read this text but the similarities of language and the spiritual attitude towards poverty are most striking. As the Bull of Canonisation says:

> She was above all a lover and firm supporter of poverty. She so rooted it in her spirit, so fixed it in her desires that, firmer in love of it and more ardent in its embrace, she never departed from her stronger and delightful union with it for any necessity.[124]

It was not only the papal text which used such language. In her first letter to Agnes of Bohemia (a letter which is still rather like one written by a noble woman living a long way away to one of whom she had only recently heard) Clare herself says:

> O blessed poverty, who bestows eternal riches on those who love and embrace her!
>
> O holy poverty, God promises the kingdom of heaven and, beyond any doubt, reveals eternal glory and blessed life to those who have and embrace her!
>
> O God-centred poverty, whom the Lord Jesus Christ, who ruled and still rules heaven and earth, who spoke and things were made, came down to embrace before all else![125]

Poverty, which appears to people as a sad state is for Clare a source of blessedness and happiness. Here we are not speaking about a monastic virtue, practised as an exercise in mortification, but of an existential discovery which far outstrips the bounds of justice. That which appears sad is instead a source of joy, that which appeared weak is instead an option of the Omnipotent Himself.

This text is so concentrated that it has no parallel, even in the writings of Francis. As has been noted, Clare speaks of poverty in her writings far more often than Francis does in his. The reasons lie in the difficult history of San Damiano community.

The legend of Clare, in the chapter dedicated to poverty, speaks about a special initiative taken by Clare and which would have been addressed to the pope:

> She asked a privilege of poverty of Innocent III of happy memory, desiring that her Order be known by the title of poverty. This magnificent man, congratulating such great a fervour in the virgin, spoke of the uniqueness of her proposal since such a privilege had never been made by the Apostolic See. The Pope himself with great joy wrote with his own hand the first draft of the privilege [that was] sought after, so that an unusual favour might smile upon an unusual request.[126]

This incident has recently been much discussed by historians. In fact, for quite some time it has been thought that the text of this 'Privilege of Poverty' in the redaction of Innocent III, had been lost. However, the French edition of the *Scritti* of Clare, published in the 'Sources Chretiennes' series in 1985 and edited by M.-F. Becker, Th. Matura and J.-F. Godet, includes in an Appendix, the text of the Privilege of Poverty in the version of Innocent III, based, it was said, 'on known manuscripts'.[127] On the basis of this, quite a number of studies have welcomed the published text as a document of great interest. Ten years later, though, in the course of a very detailed study, Werner Malaczek published a learned text with the title *Das 'Privilegium paupertatis' Innocenz III. und das Testament der Klara von Assisi*.[128] In this he decisively adopts a position against the authenticity of the text published in 'Sources chretiennes'. The author, a specialist in documents of the thirteenth century Roman Curia, particularises a number of expressions which do not conform to the usage of the Chancellery. His conclusions are absolutely convincing, with the proviso that in all the codices cited we are talking of a privilege of poverty from Innocent but without specifying Innocent III.

A further but indirect confirmation comes from Br Mariano of Florence, a friar minor who lived at the turn of the fifteenth and sixteenth centuries. It was he who composed the *Libro della degnità et excellentiae del ordine della seraphica madre delle povere donne sancta Chiara da Assisi*.[129] This text, as the title indicates, is a collection of all the testimonies and documents concerning the Order which takes it origin from Clare. If Mariano had even so much as suspected that Innocent III had written a privilege of poverty, he would certainly had mentioned it, especially since it would then have been the oldest pontifical document in the history of Franciscanism. Instead, Mariano simply says: 'this rule which St Francis gave to St Clare has been confirmed with privileges and approved by more than one supreme pontiff.'[130]

So what are we to think of this statement in the Legend of St Clare? First, it must be said that the text does not suggest a personal meeting between Clare and the pope himself. In fact, the whole Legend always underlines enclosure as a dimension of the life of Clare and would not have been able to contravene it in this particular case without a more explicit reference. It is also certain that the testimony comes from an eye witness account, which records the amazement of the pope at such an unusual request. The same witness underlines then the great joy with which Innocent himself set to and wrote a *notula* a 'minute' to the privilege itself. To this, Malaczek notes that the 'term used here, *notula* for 'minute' in a papal letter does not correspond to the usage customary in the papal chancellery which would have been a *nota* or *littera notata'*.[131]

Therefore the text of the Legend does not necessarily refer to a juridical document drawn up by Innocent III. Here, though, we recall the passage in the Testament of Clare in which she says:

> Moreover, for greater security, I took care to have our profession of the most holy poverty that we promised our father strengthened with privileges by the Lord Pope Innocent in whose time we had our beginning, and by his other successors, that we would never in any way turn away from her.[132]

This is one of the principle reasons why Malaczek also denies the authenticity of Clare's Testament. Perhaps though, it is not necessary to come to quite so radical a conclusion. First of all, if the thirteenth century dating of one of the manuscripts which preserve the text can be demonstrated, then the Testament remains as having a certain relevance—leaving aside whether it be authentically by Clare or a forged work of someone obviously close to her. This situation would be strengthened if the text can be confirmed by another source. In reality, of course, the Testament does not speak of a *privilege of poverty* of Innocent III. Clare only says that she had recourse to that pope and to his successors to gain confirmation of her choice of poverty, to receive privileges from them. Moreover, because the text published in the Sources Chretiennes is attributed to Innocent IV in some manuscripts, one could maintain that the Testament is referring to the privilege granted by Gregory IX and noted by Innocent IV.

Assessing the data we have, we could suggest the following development of the problem of a juridical protection of poverty on Clare's part: in the beginning at San Damiano they lived Franciscan poverty with the same radicality as the first brothers, as described in the *Regula non Bullata* but without any juridical guarantee. In the second stage, there is no reason to think that Clare would have gone so far as personally to present a request for recognition of such a form of poverty to Innocent III. It has recently been suggested that the pope might have been enchanted by such a request, that what he personally would have written was certainly not a formal *minute* to such a document but more simply a first draft, a *notula*, a note without any juridical value. Perhaps he drafted what was a *divertissement* to any legal expert, a privilege in which he affirmed the right not to be constrained to have privileges.[133] So we are certainly speaking of an approval here, but one without any juridical validity, exactly as happened to Francis' Rule for the brothers which was granted only verbal approval.

If this hypothesis is found to be correct, something would have happened for Clare parallel to what happened to that woman accused of incest who was brought into the presence of Innocent III during a consistory, that is a meeting of the Pope and his cardinals, somewhere in 1216. According to the account of Cesarius of Hesterbach, this woman 'with great importunity pushed her way into the presence of my Lord Pope Innocent and made her confession before everyone present, with so many tears and regrets that everyone was amazed. My lord the Pope, seeing the woman's great contrition and that she was truly penitent, was moved with mercy towards her. Like a shrewd doctor, wanting to heal her infirmity quickly and thoroughly, and wanting also to test her out with the medicine of contrition, ordered that she be dressed as she had been when she had sinned. The woman had come in dressed only in her shift. The Pope, 'considering that no stain of sin could resist such an obedience allied to such modesty and to such penitence said, before them all: Your sins are forgiven you, go in peace.'[134]

It is not possible to know whether Innocent's actual text was also preserved at San Damiano. What is certain is that no less a person than Gregory IX construed the behaviour of this great pope as a precedent which could not be ignored when, some years later, Clare sought to obtain a true document with full juridical force, namely the *privilegium paupertatis* in the redaction which we know today.

However, this does not solve all the problems. Innocent IV, also wanted to write a rule for the Order of which San Damiano was part. In this, for the first time, the link with the Order of Friars Minor would be affirmed explicitly. On the other hand, he also said:

> You may be permitted to receive, to have in common and freely to retain produce and possessions. A procurator, one who is prudent as well as loyal, may be had in every monastery of the Order to deal with these possessions in a becoming way.[135]

This was an explicit denial of the option for absolute poverty which Clare promised to Francis. Because of all this, towards the end of her life, Clare decided to complete this journey by writing a rule for her sisters herself. In order to gain approval for this, she had to go through the Cardinal Protector, Rainaldo of Jenne, bishop of Ostia. The Legend tells us:

> The Lord of Ostia, after hearing about the increase of her sickness, hurried from Perugia to visit the spouse of Christ. He had become a father to her by his office, a provider by his care, always a dedicated friend by his very pure affection. He nourished the sick woman with the Sacrament of the Body of the Lord, and fed those remaining with the encouragement of his salutary word.

Then she begged so great a father with her tears to take care of her soul and those of the other Ladies for the name of Christ. but, above all, she asked him to petition to have the Privilege of Poverty confirmed by the Lord Pope and the Cardinals. Because he was a faithful helper of the Order, just as he promised by his word, so he fulfilled in his deed.[136]

This passage is always interpreted by commentators as referring to the Rule of Clare itself but the writer is clearly speaking of the Privilege of Poverty. In effect, this would exactly correspond to the text of the privilege erroneously attributed to Innocent III, because in that there is a phrase (the only difference from the text of Gregory IX) which says:

If any woman does not wish to, or cannot observe a proposal of this sort, *(propositum)* let her not have a dwelling place among you, but let her be transferred to another place.[137]

This phrase would have made no sense to the young community at the time of Innocent III when all the sisters at San Damiano knew very well what a radical proposal of poverty they would be undertaking. It fits the context of the middle of the century, though, when quite a number of the monasteries had no clear concept of the poverty of Clare and as a result she needed to foresee the possibility that, if a community sought to adhere to the *privilegium paupertatis*, then those who could not or who did not want to, had the option of transferring elsewhere.

The testimony of Sr Filippa di Leonardo di Gislerio at the canonisation process turns on this theme of the privilege obtained by Clare during the last days of her life:

At the end of her life, after calling together all her sisters, she entrusted the Privilege of Poverty to them. Her great desire was to have the *Form of Life* of the Order confirmed with a papal bull, to be able one day to place her lips upon the papal seal and then, on the following day, to die. It occurred just as she desired.[138]

Once again, commentators have interpreted the words of Filippa as a confusion between the Privilege of Poverty and the Rule. The awareness that there was a text of the Privilege in existence granted by Innocent IV, makes it likely that the sister was not mistaken. On the contrary, there would have been two papal bulls delivered to San Damiano on the day before Clare's death. One contained the approval of the Rule ad the other the famous Privilege.

The struggle to have the *privilegium paupertatis* recognised had come to an end for Clare although only on her deathbed. If this had been the way things unfolded, it would explain why Alexander IV, who was none other than the Cardinal Rainaldo who had personally undertaken to seek the approval of the Privilege from his predecessor Innocent IV, said of her in the Bull of Canonisation that she was 'endowed here below with the privilege of the most exalted poverty.'[139]

· · · · · · · ·

ASYMMETRICAL
SYMMETRY:
CLARE AND
FRANCIS

What was the relationship between
Clare and Francis really like? Someone has said that

> in meeting Clare, Francis found the feminine side of himself, his
> tenderness, and in that relationship with Francis, Clare found the
> masculine side of herself, her strength. Each of them chased fear
> away from the other. Francis no longer had any fear of being ten-
> der and thus became strong. Clare, through her relationship with
> Francis, developed her own tenderness and thus became strong.
> Francis rediscovered his masculinity in Clare, his strength, and
> Clare found her femininity in Francis, her nourishment, her ten-
> derness.[140]

This seems all very beautiful but what basis has it in the sources? If
we look at the text of the *Legend*, it strikes us that Francis was not
often there.

> Clare, in the reconstruction of sources—and perhaps in reality
> too—is still linked to the monastic tradition of the preceding cen-
> tury. And the presence of Francis was only a presence: in the offi-
> cial story of Clare, Francis does not aspire to be a model.[141]

So what was the importance of Clare in Francis' life and the importance of Francis in Clare's life?

In the *Regula non Bullata*, which sums up the primitive experience of the *minorite fraternity*, it says:

> Wherever they may be or may go, let all the brothers avoid evil glances and association with women. No one may counsel them, travel alone with them or eat out of the same dish with them.[142]

And a little later it says:

> Absolutely no woman may be received to obedience by any brother, but after spiritual advice has been given to her, let her do penance wherever she wants.[143]

This seems to leave no room for doubt: Francis, right from the beginning of his experience, did not want women associates in any way, nor did he want to 'receive them to obedience'.

The situation begins to grow complicated however, when we look at the Rule of Clare where it says:

> Clare, the unworthy handmaid of Christ and the little plant of the most blessed Father Francis, promises obedience and reverence to the Lord Pope Innocent and his successors canonically elected, and to the Roman Church. And just as at the beginning she promised obedience to the Blessed Francis, so now she promises to observe the same inviolably to his successors.[144]

Here Clare affirms—and in open contradiction to the *Regula non Bullata*—that on the contrary, she and her sisters were received to obedience by Francis himself. We have here an affirmation which might sound strange, so much so that Clare herself felt the need to state it again in the sixth chapter of her Rule:

After the Most High Heavenly Father saw fit by his grace to enlighten my heart to do penance according to the example and teaching of our most blessed father Saint Francis, shortly after his own conversion, I, together with my sisters, willingly promised him obedience.[145]

If we widen our glance to include the writings of both Francis and Clare, we cannot help being struck by 'this brutal fact: Clare who mentions Francis thirty-two times in her works, is never named in his'[146] The credit for having noted this imbalance belongs to Jacques Delarun:

> The relationship between the father and his little plant is extremely asymmetrical. This does not stop us understanding the fascination which Francis had for Clare, rather the contrary. In any rapport between human beings, the most vibrant dynamic will be found in disequilibrium.[147]

The conclusion is even tighter: The most dangerous trap is that of a false effect of symmetry between Francis and Clare which does not, in fact, withstand even a first examination.

In the Conclusion to his own volume, Giovanni Miccoli comments:

> There is amazement rather than judgment: starting with the text the result is elementary, I would even say obvious in its stark simplicity. So far, however, nobody has shown sufficient awareness to enable them to draw conclusions from their research. Sugary pages about some mystical couple that never existed, all evaporate, but instead another style of discourse imposes itself. This is because, if it is obvious that Francis was wholly supportive of Clare's lifestyle and religious choices, then we have nothing specific in the

'opuscula', the writings of Francis, on which to base this, or not if we are looking at Francis' specific attitude towards her.[148]

This conclusion leads us to postulate that Francis had great importance for Clare but that Clare did not have an equivalent importance for Francis. However, this is not an entirely new observation. Bonaventure himself noted this imbalance and, in the *Legenda Maior* inserts a second episode in which Francis was, at a particular point, overwhelmed by doubts about his vocation:

> What do you think, brothers, what do you judge better? That I should spend my time in prayer, or that I should travel about preaching? [...] When he had mulled over these words for many days with his brothers, he could not perceive with certainty which of these he should choose as more acceptable to Christ. [...] Choosing, therefore, two of the brothers, he sent them to Brother Sylvester, who had seen the cross coming out of his mouth, and at that time spent his time in continuous prayer on the mountain above Assisi. He was to ask God to resolve his doubt over this matter and to send him the answer in God's name. He also asked the holy virgin Clare to consult with the purest and simplest of the virgins living under her rule, and to pray herself with the other sisters in order to seek the Lord's will in this matter. Through a miraculous revelation of the Spirit, the venerable priest and the virgin dedicated to God came to the same conclusion: that it was the divine good will that the herald of Christ should preach.[149]

Here we have an incident being used, and wisely, by Bonaventure in order to highlight his balanced understanding of the Franciscan charism: two contemplatives (Sylvester and Clare) were charged by God himself to communicate to Francis his will that Francis give himself to the active life. Bonaventure's testimony is undoubtedly a late one given that we find no sign of such an episode in any of the preceding Lives, either of Francis or of Clare. However, Bonaventure's voice on a subject so debated within the Order cannot be taken lightly. It is probably not without reason that an episode in which Clare assumes the role of a guide to Francis, only surfaced after her death in 1253. In fact, as far as we can tell from her writings, Clare did not like to speak of herself at all and therefore hid behind the memory of Francis, but after her death her sisters would have had no problem about recounting such an incident in order to underline the bonds which bound the sisters to the brothers. The observation that there is no mention of this incident in the Canonisation Process does not carry much weight, since at the Canonisation Process they were called to give evidence about the holiness of Clare, while this incident could be thought of as pertaining more to the holiness of Francis.

In any case, whether the incident was 'invented' by Bonaventure, or transmitted by the sisters at San Damiano via Brother Leo (to whom Bonaventure turned at the beginning of his time as General in order to learn about Clare and her companions) or whether the account is historical fact, it remains as evidence that a few years after Clare's death, the Minister General of the Order of Friars Minor wanted to underline the importance of Clare in the life of Francis. It is difficult to say any more about the importance of Clare in Francis' life. It is true, as we have already noted, that in the *Legend of Saint Clare* Francis appears occasionally and that these occasions refer mainly to the earlier times of Clare's religious life. However, this silence in the *Legend* is amply made up for by the Acts of the Process of Canonisation.

Sister Filippa di Leonardo di Gislerio, the third witness at the process, says, at a certain point in her testimony:

Lady Clare also related how once in a vision, it seemed to her she brought a bowl of hot water to Saint Francis along with a towel for drying his hands. She was climbing a very high stairway, but was going very quickly, almost as though she were going on level ground. When she reached Saint Francis, the saint bared his breast and said to the Lady Clare: Come, take and drink. After she had sucked from it, the saint admonished her to imbibe once again. After she did so what she had tasted was so sweet and delightful she in no way could describe it. After she had imbibed, that nipple or opening of the breast from which the milk comes remained between the lips of blessed Clare. After she took was remained in her mouth in her hands, it seemed to her it was gold so clear and bright that everything was seen in it as in a mirror.[150]

The *Legend* makes no mention of any such vision. The matter may have seemed too sensitive to put into a text written for the edification of young women who wanted to choose religious life. Indeed, some of the sisters at the Canonisation process, people like sister Amata, referred to the same vision where she says:

> She said the same as Sister Filippa concerning all these things: the miracle of Saint Clare's mother, her vision and the breast of Saint Francis, the miracle of the night of the Lord's Nativity.[151]

Obviously Clare did not tell only one sister about her vision, but she told all those who were living with her. These in their turn, during the process, did not forget to tell about it as among the notable events of Clare's life. It seems that the vision did not cause any embarrassment either to Clare or to the other sisters at San Damiano. Rather the contrary, for the sisters, it demonstrated the holiness of their mother.

Through the witness of Filippa, we touch something which was an aspect of medieval monastic culture, although, probably for lack of material, it has not been much studied. This is the question of how, and in what way did women give themselves to the salvation of souls. How did they preach, instruct and share their personal mystical experiences with them and even their dreams?[152]

What seems strange here is the fact that Clare did not speak with her sisters about her relationship with Christ but her relationship with Francis. However, if we look closely the matter it is not as a strange as it seems at first. In all probability the vision took place after the death of Francis, given that Sister Amata, who mentions it in her evidence, did not enter until after 1228 or 1229. In that case we are dealing with a period of great uncertainty for the community at San Damiano. As we have seen the loss of Francis was followed by a considerable pressure being applied to Clare to renounce some of those elements of her religious experience which she considered fundamental, namely poverty and her link with the friars. Obviously, in these circumstances Clare and her sisters would have looked back to the one who had been their strong support, even though the blessed father was now dead.[153]

The vision appears as a consolation, a divine response to her need. In the details of everyday life such as a towel or a basin of water, Clare could see in that very everydayness that there was a path upwards through the weariness of life at San Damiano. There at the summit Francis awaited her and the ascent seemed to her very easy. When she reached Francis, he gave her his own milk to drink. The fact that the saint was presented as in a feminine body did not pose any problem to Clare or to the other sisters. It is obvious that what is being expressed here is the spiritual maternity of Francis who gives Clare something to drink and nourishes her and thereby recognises her as a daughter. For her this was an experience of happiness: it was so sweet and delightful that there was no way she could explain it.

Then, however, the dream had an unexpected development: after she had drunk,

> what she had tasted was so sweet and delightful she in no way could describe it. After she had imbibed, that nipple or opening of the breast from which the milk comes remained between the lips of blessed Clare.[154]

In other words, a part of the body of Francis, a part of Francis himself remained with Clare. Finally, after she took what remained in her mouth in her hands, it seemed to her it was gold so clear and bright that everything was seen in it as in a mirror. Clare had not only interiorised a part of Francis, but she herself had been transformed; her image and stature were the equal of Francis'. She herself through her dream had been transformed into a mirror of Francis, into another Francis. This then is the concrete significance which the vision must have had for the sisters of San Damiano. Confronted by any questions about who was their support after the death of Francis, the dream responds that it was Clare herself who had now been transformed into another Francis and that she would now be all the support they might need. This too is the reason why the sisters tell about the vision during the Canonisation process.

Just this dream on its own would be enough to demonstrate the depth and spiritual liberty which characterized the rapport between Clare and Francis. To this we can add the expressions used by Clare in her Rule where, abandoning legal formality, she defines herself most warmly as the 'unworthy handmaid of Christ and the little plant of the most blessed father Francis'.[155] We must not forget that here, as in the account of her vision, Clare is speaking of Francis some time after his death. So here too their relationship seems asymmetrical since from the time of Francis' death in 1226 until her own death in 1253, she transformed herself into a watchful witness of the blessed father's memory.

Clare, a witness to Francis

For over twenty-seven years, Clare survived the man who had persuaded her to leave everything in order, as a poor woman, to follow the poor Christ. Throughout these twenty-seven years she preserved and defended—sometimes not without difficulty—the ideal of life which she had learnt from Francis himself. These same twenty-seven years were also among the most dramatic in the history of the Franciscan movement. These were the years of beginning to build the basilica in Assisi while, simultaneously, Brother Elias became more and more alienated. They were the years of the canonisation of Francis but also the years of *Quo elongati* and of what has been described as the transition from 'intuition to institution'.

Throughout this time, Clare was not an isolated onlooker but one of the protagonists who determined and influenced the development of this religious movement which Francis had set in motion. Her prestige at the heart of the Order must have been considerable if we reflect that it was to her that Gregory IX himself went with great respect, and she who was, at the same time, in easy contact with Brother Elias as well as with Leo, Angelo and the other companions.

There is an incident which is related in one of the secondary sources which perhaps typifies the way in which the Franciscan movement had come to value Clare's role as custodian of Francis' memory. This source is the Life of Brother Giles, in which we are told that once a very learned brother had been invited to preach at San Damiano. While he was speaking, Brother Giles interrupted him and replaced him as the one speaking to the sisters. At the end, he returned the speaker's role to the learned brother who, most humbly, then concluded his sermon. Clare, observing all this, exclaimed: 'This is like seeing Francis himself again!'[156] According to this account, Clare had secured the best of the brothers to preach to her sisters, even though he had come from a long way off. Following the thread of the narrative further, it emerges that Brother Giles was also very familiar with San Damiano and that the preacher was listened to by him together with the sisters. Finally, the narrative reveals the role of Clare who did not preach but who gave a clear testimony, looking back to the memory of Francis. In a certain sense, it does not matter where the account tells of something that really happened. The significant thing is that very diverse sources attribute to San Damiano this role of holding the memory, and that they see Clare as the custodian of that memory.

The role of 'custodian of the memory' which Clare chose for herself, also revealed itself in a number of ways—as has already been said—in the years which followed the deposition of Brother Elias, years when the order felt a need to gather other direct testimonies of their founder in order to reconstruct a different hagiographic profile. The years 1244–1246 were difficult years during which the history of the memory of Francis of Assisi was definitively constructed. A simple examination of the various compilations which, from the end of the thirteenth century to the beginning of the fourteenth, contested the authenticity of the various memories, reveal that what was at stake was not simply the image of the seraphic father, but more comprehensively, the very identity of the Franciscan Order.

The General Chapter of the Order of Friars Minor was held at Genoa on 4 October 1244. The newly-elected Minister General, Crescentius of Iesi, invited all the brothers to send in their personal memories with a view to making a new *Life of Francis of Assisi*. This would satisfy the devout and legitimate curiosity of everyone and, at the same time, complement in various ways, the first official biography. The invitation, or better the injunction, was sent to all the brothers but, quite logically, it was directed more at the surviving companions of Francis. Among those who had been with him the longest, were certainly Leo, Rufino and Angelo. We learn from the famous letter written from Greccio on 11 August 1246, that the three closest disciples responded to the invitation and also included the memories of Filippo, Illuminato and Masseo. The testimonies of Giles and Bernard had been gathered up by the evidence of a (not clearly identified) Brother John, Giovanni, who was a companion of those two followers of Francis. The material thus gathered was used by Thomas of Celano in his redaction of the *Vita Secunda*, the second Life as is clear from many other testimonies. Part of that material, as is again well known, then found its definitive place in unofficial Franciscan compilations and collections.

In all this work of remembering, even if in contradiction, Clare would not have been absent. Certainly she made Thomas of Celano, in the process of writing his *Vita Secunda*, aware of the text of that note which Francis had sent to the sisters of San Damiano. At the same time, as we saw in Chapter One, other memories seem to have come from the community of Clare. In all probability, it was this group of testimonies which told the story about Francis and the Crucifix, as well as the prophecy the saint had made about the birth at San Damiano of a community of virgins. Side by side with these, though, there are other episodes which begin to appear in the compilations from more or less the same period, beginning with Francis first begging and his shame at going into a house where he was known in order to beg oil for a lamp to burn before the image of the crucifix:

One day the man of God was going through Assisi begging oil to fill the lamps in the church of San Damiano, which he was then rebuilding. He saw a crowd carousing by the house he intended to enter. Turning bright red, he backed away. But then, turning his noble spirit towards heaven, he rebuked his cowardice and called himself to account. He went back immediately to the house and frankly explained to them what had made him ashamed. Then, as if drunk in the Spirit, he spoke in French and asked for oil and he got it.[157]

Another of those incidents was the preaching with ashes:

> While the holy father was staying at San Damiano, he was pestered by his vicar with repeated requests that he should present the word of God to his daughters, and he finally gave in to his insistence. The Ladies gathered as usual to hear the word of God, but no less to see their father, and he raised his eyes to heaven where he always had his heart, and began to pray to Christ. Then he had ashes brought and made a circle with them round himself on the floor, and then put the rest on his own head. As they waited, the blessed father remained in silence within the circle of ashes, and real amazement grew in their hearts. Suddenly, he got up and to their great surprise, recited the *Have mercy on me God* instead of a sermon. As he finished it, he left quickly.[158]

This is another incident which can only have come from Clare. The place, San Damiano, the choice of the term 'daughters' to indicate the sisters, the very originality of Francis' behaviour, so filled with echoes not only of the penitent mentality but also of the popular culture, make us think of this account as an eye witness testimony, and one which across so many years, can only have come from Clare.

This aspect of memory is another aspect of the asymmetrical symmetry between Francis and Clare. While we always think Clare can only be understood in the light of Francis, looking at the sources leads us to the contrary conclusion and that for us, today, it is possible to know some aspects of the life of Francis only in the light of Clare's testimony.

CHAPTER
EIGHT

'DAMIANITES',
POOR SISTERS
OR POOR LADIES
ENCLOSED?

'Between silence and memory'—
towards the end of her life, this seems to have been Clare's position
in the Franciscan movement. It was a silence which would confine
her to the official writings of the Order along with the memory of
Francis which she defended so tenaciously. But what was Clare's
position at the heart of the other women's communities which had
arisen everywhere, beginning in central Italy? In other words, what
was not only the personal position of Clare but what was the position of the community of San Damiano at the heart of those
women's religious communities which, in pontifical documents, had
come to be called the *Order of San Damiano*?

If we look at the register of Gregory IX, we are astounded at the
number of documents which refer to these women's communities. It
is possible that the pope had interested himself in these groups of
women who, until about ten years earlier, had been directed and
advised by the men's branch of the Order or by the diocesan bishops. The pope's interest, as has been said, began some years earlier
while he was still a cardinal, and in the course of his work as legate

in central Italy. Then he had promoted and protected the birth of the early experience of the same Order.

In March, 1218, in the name of the Apostolic See, Cardinal Hugolino accepted the donation of some land on the hill of Monticelli near Florence. On this hill were to live a group of women who wanted to live a religious life in community. On 18 July in that same year, the same cardinal accepted from a certain Glotto di Monaldo the donation of land at Monteluce near Perugia. Two weeks later the bishop of that city granted a group of women religious who had established themselves on that land, exemption from the taxes due to the ordinary or bishop, apart from an annual pound of wax.

At this point, the cardinal went back to the pope to gain authorisation to place monasteries directly under the Apostolic See from the time of their foundation.[159]

In the letter which he sent to these women religious and which was later confirmed by the Pope Honorius III, Hugolino said:

> Lest the assault of rash temerity make them abandon or falter in their pious purpose (which God forbid) we must offer our protection to those prudent virgins who, in the habit of religious life, prepare themselves to go with lighted lamps to meet the bridegroom, and by the way of holiness to enter with him into the heavenly bridal chamber.[160]

Given that the prevailing biblical image under which women's monasticism appears most frequently in papal letters is that of the prudent virgins, Hugolino had not imagined anything. In fact, the cardinal developed and carried forward with particular wisdom, an explicit policy of the pontifical Curia since the time of Innocent III, which was that of directly binding religious communities, especially those of women, to the Apostolic See. The groups of women from Florence and Perugia, and also some from Siena and Lucca, were gathered by Hugolino under Roman protection, but these groups are the clearest examples of a passage from simple protection to the more explicit submission of such religious ventures to the authority of the Roman pontiff.

During the next year, the cardinal himself drew up some Constitutions, based on the Rule of St Benedict which were to be observed by the new communities of women which Hugolino was promoting. The heart of that rule (or Constitutions) is the option of enclosure, as he says right at the beginning: [the nuns] must remain enclosed the whole time of their life.[161]

In this way was born—even juridically—the *Religio pauperum dominarum de Valle Spoleti sive Tuscia,* or the Congregation of the poor Ladies of the valley of Spoleto or of Tuscany. This was the first time in the history of the Roman Catholic Church that an order had been created which was entirely for women and with no masculine branch which took responsibility for them.

The solution of Hugolino was himself to retain the direction of the entire *religio* [or Order] as Cardinal if not as founder, given that they lacked a precise institutional point of reference and consequently any guidance.[162]

What did all this have to do with the group of women gathered around Clare at San Damiano? Little or nothing. Unlike those of Perugia, Florence, Siena or Lucca, Clare's community had not been born as the result of any interest on the part of a prelate. It had come into being, as we have seen, through the initiative of Clare herself and through the preaching of Francis, with the probable kindness of Bishop Guido on whom the little church of San Damiano was juridically dependent.

Very soon, however, Hugolino came into contact with Francis and then with Clare. This is shown by a letter from him addressed to 'his very dear sister in Christ and mother of his salvation, Lady Clare.'[163] This was written immediately after his stay near San Damiano, probably in the spring of 1220. In spite of the period's redundancies of style, the tone of this letter allows an admiration to come through which appears sincere:

> From that very hour when the necessity of returning here separated me from your holy conversation and tore me away from that joy of heavenly treasure, such a bitterness of heart, such an abundance of tears and such an immensity of sorrow have overcome me that [...] although I have always known and considered myself to be a sinner, yet after having recognised a sure sign of your merits and having observed the rigour of your life, I have learned with certainty that I have [...] so offended the Lord of the whole universe that I am not worthy to be freed from earthly concerns and be associated with the company of the elect unless your prayers and tears obtain for me pardon for my sins.[164]

So it is not without foundation that the *Legend* says:

> Not without reason, Lord Pope Gregory had marvellous faith in the prayers of this holy woman whose efficacious power he had experienced. Frequently when some new difficulties arose, as is natural, both when he was Bishop of Ostia and later when he was elevated to the Apostolic See, he would request assistance of that virgin by means of a letter and would experience her help.[165]

All this admiration explains why Hugolino very soon wanted to make San Damiano the centre and heart of this Order which he himself had instituted, and perhaps to entrust them all to the care of the Friars Minor. This project took some years to realise, partly because until the approval of the rule in 1223, Francis was unable to assume the pastoral care of nuns. The change came in 1226 with the death of Francis and the ascent to the papal throne of Hugolino, taking the name of Gregory IX.

The elderly pope immediately found himself locked in conflict with the Emperor, Frederick II, and in tackling all the difficulties of this he put great trust in the prayers of the nuns. As he wrote in a letter to Benedetta, abbess of the monastery of Santa Maria in Siena and to her sisters:

> We ask and beg in the Lord Jesus that there come from your heart a constant cry to the Lord, so that the servant of the Servants of Christ and above all your servant and that of all the handmaids of the Lord, might not be overwhelmed by a sea of storms.[166]

A little while later the pope wrote to Clare, commanding her to become part of the Order which he had instituted. The heart of the letter concerns life in the enclosure:

> ... because you are bound to love your Bridegroom above all other things [...] so that, with all your affections, you must delight only in him in order that nothing can succeed in separating you from his love. With this in view, then, and divinely inspired, you will remain enclosed in the cloister so that, with the saving grace of abdicating from the world and everything in it, you may embrace your Bridegroom with an uncorrupted heart, running to him in the fragrance of his perfumes.[167]

The pope was well aware that Clare would not easily accept the obedience of such a command and so he adds:

If indeed, as we trust and hope with certainty, you will consider these matters carefully and diligently, then those things which now appear bitter to you will be turned into saving sweetness, those which are hard will become easy and the harsh become soft so that you will be able to glory if you have merited to suffer something for Christ who underwent the passion of a despised death for us.

In July that year the pope went to Assisi for the canonisation of Francis, and this was when he met with Clare at San Damiano, during which meeting the pope proposed that he absolve her from her vow of poverty so that she could accept some income, and he receives the famous riposte:

> Holy Father, I will never in any way wish to be absolved from the following of Christ.[168]

The pope did not insist as regards poverty but all the same he went ahead with his project of creating one single order of all religious women. On 18 August 1228 there is a letter from Cardinal Rainaldo directed to various religious communities of women in Italy, informing them that the Pope had named him the Cardinal Protector of the new Order. The relevant thing is that the first of the twenty-four communities named is San Damiano of Assisi.[169]

This assimilation of the San Damiano community into the other groups of religious women must have considerably concerned Clare, so much so that in fact, on 17 September in that same year, she obtained the famous *Privilegium Paupertatis*, the Privilege of Poverty. This was the privilege of not being obliged to receive privileges, the right to live without any rights, the guarantee of living without guarantees. The text itself is very expressive:

> Gregory, Bishop, Servant of the servants of God, to his beloved daughters in Christ, Clare and the other servants of Christ gath-

ered together in the church of San Damiano in the diocese of Assisi, health and apostolic benediction.

As is evident, you have renounced the desire for all temporal things, desiring to dedicate yourselves to the Lord alone. Because of this, since you have sold all things and given them to the poor, you propose not to have any possessions whatsoever, clinging in all things to the footprints of Him, the Way, the Truth and the Life, who for our sake was made poor. Nor does a lack of possessions frighten you from a proposal of this sort; for the left hand of the heavenly Spouse is under your head to support the weakness of your body, which you have placed under the law of your soul through an ordered charity. Finally, he who feeds the birds of the heavens and clothes the lilies of the field will not fail you in either food or clothing, until he ministers to you in heaven, when his right hand especially will more happily embrace you in the fullness of his sight. Therefore we confirm with our apostolic authority, as you requested, your proposal of most high poverty, granting you by the authority of those present that no one can compel you to receive possessions.

Therefore let no one be permitted to tamper with this document of our concession or dare to oppose it with rash temerity. If anyone shall presume to attempt this, let him know that he will incur the wrath of Almighty God and his blessed apostles, Peter and Paul.[170]

At this point Clare found herself holding a preeminent position in the religious congregation founded by Hugolino but thanks to this document she was able to guarantee the originality of her own project at San Damiano.

However, the institutional journey of the new order was far from finished. Gregory IX continued to concern himself personally in these women's communities, even though he had appointed Rainaldo as cardinal protector. On 2 December 1234, he wrote another letter, this time addressing it to:

> His beloved daughters in Christ, the Abbess and Enclosed Nuns of the Order of Saint Damian of Assisi, health and apostolic blessing.[171]

With this, it could be said that the pope's project had come into being. For the first time, those who had once been called *The Poor Ladies of the Valley of Spoleto* were now named the Order of San Damiano.

Within this group of communities, however, some communities wanted to profess a particular form of life which they modelled quite specifically on that of San Damiano. This meant that they had difficulties with the directives of Gregory IX. The best known example is that of the monastery in Prague. The correspondence between Clare and Agnes of Bohemia shows us very clearly the level of friendship and, if you will, of complicity of the two women in obtaining permission from Gregory IX for them to live in Prague as they did at San Damiano. At first the pope seemed to concede, granting Prague a text similar to the Privilege of Poverty. This is the letter *Pia credulitate tenentes* of 16 April 1238, which says among other things:

> you who have contemned things visible in order to hasten to the delights of things unseen, are desirous of avoiding that obstacle— which is accustomed to arise—to a contemplation of God, which is unhampered by the care of temporal things. Therefore overcome by your petitions and tears, we grant by the authority of this letter that you cannot be unwillingly forced to accept any possessions from this time on.[172]

However, when Agnes (probably in conjunction with Clare) was bold enough to want to follow in Prague that observance, the *observantiae regulares,* which Francis had given to the sisters at San Damiano, the pope replied that there was no way he could grant such a thing. He redefined the institutional contours of the monastery of Assisi:

> Surely, O daughter of benediction and grace, when we were yet established in a lesser office and that beloved daughter in Christ, Clare, the Abbess of the Monastery of Saint Damian in Assisi, and certain other devout women in the Lord cast aside worldly vanity and chose to serve him under the yoke of religious observance, Blessed Francis gave them, as newborn children, not solid food but rather a milk drink, a formula of life, which seemed to be suited for them. This formula of life was presented to us in writing some time ago by our beloved son, the Prior of Saint Francis' Hospice in Prague, a man who is at all times discerning and concerned about your goal. With humble supplication he asked us to see to it that the form of life, presented to us by him under your seal and constructed from the existing formula of life plus certain chapters which are contained in the Rule of the Order of Saint Damian, be confirmed by apostolic authority.
>
> Having recourse to prudent deliberation, we did not for various reasons deem it expedient to give it the full stamp of approval.

The pope gave four reasons for this:

> First, because Clare and her sisters had the privilege of exemption which was given to them by Pope Honorius at our request and they solemnly professed that Rule which was composed with careful zeal and accepted by St Francis and afterwards confirmed by the same Pope Honorius, our predecessor of happy memory.

Secondly because Clare and her sisters put aside the formula and have been observing the same Rule in a laudable manner from the time of their profession until the present.

Thirdly, because it has been determined that this Rule be uniformly observed everywhere by those who profess it, and because grave and insupportable scandal could arise by assuming what is contrary to it.

This is especially so since other sisters of this Order put aside the formula and have been observing the same Rule, seeing the integrity of the Rule violated, may with disturbed hearts waver in its observance. God forbid![173]

Confronted with the *formula vitae* of Francis as well as the Rule written by him, the pope commented that only the second had received any legal approval (from Honorius III) and that therefore only this second document could be the basis for the life of the nuns in Prague. Agnes was obliged to submit even though she did not entirely abandon the hope of coming into line with the praxis of life at San Damiano.

The wheel of life, however, has some unexpected turns. Three years later Gregory IX had to write a letter to all the archbishops and bishops, in which he made clear his disapproval that there were further causes for lament concerning *nonnullae mulieres*, certain women in various dioceses who were asserting, falsely, that they belonged to the Order of San Damiano. With the intent of proving this belonging, they were going without shoes, wearing the habit and cord proper to the Order of San Damiano and were becoming known as either the Discalced or as Minoresses. However they were to be distinguished from the true Damianites by the fact that the latter lived as permanent recluses.

The existence of women who were dressing like the sisters of the Order of San Damiano while living an itinerant life must have greatly preoccupied the pontiff[174] as well as those other men responsible for the Order. These had, often against their will, assumed the *cura monialium*, the care of the nuns, of those religious who were living in enclosed monasteries. Now they found themselves obliged to confront these other women who were living the same itinerant life as themselves. It was at this time that the recollection emerged of how Francis kept his distance in confrontation with women. And it is at this time that Clare, as we have said, disappeared from the memory of the Order.[175]

Innocent IV, who succeeded Gregory IX, tried to resolve the problem by drafting a new Form of Life which was based on the Rule of St Francis and not on that of Benedict. This *form of life*, drawn up and promulgated by Innocent IV in 1247, granted

> to you and those who will come after you the observance of the Rule of Saint Francis with respect to the three things only, namely obedience, the renunciation of property in particular and chastity, as well as the *forma vivendi* according to which you have particularly decided to live, and written in this present document.[176]

In spite of this link with the Order of Friars Minor, to which she had held so tenaciously, the *forma vitae* of Innocent IV did not find favour with Clare who very soon turned her attention to her own Rule. Probably her problem was primarily the drawing back from absolute poverty by Innocent:

> ... you may be permitted to receive, to have in common and freely to retain produce and possessions. A procurator—one who is prudent as well as loyal—may be had in every monastery of the Order, to deal with these possessions in a becoming way.[177]

By the end of her life, Clare was doing something that no other woman had tried to do before her, namely to write her own Rule for herself and her sisters. To do this, she had to take into account all the other *formulae vitae* which had been given to or imposed on her. The text which emerged from this labour was a wise linking of citations, based on the *Regula bullata* of the Friars Minor. Clare also made use of the *Regula non bullata*, the *forma vitae* of Hugolino as well as demonstrating that she was familiar with the rule of Benedict and also the *forma vitae* of Innocent IV. It might be thought this was a wearisome collage of juridical texts, but that is not the case. The Rule of Clare has an element in common with all the great rules in the history of the Church: it has been written by someone who was living that which was being prescribed. Like Benedict and Augustine, Clare too did not aim for the impossible but seems guided by a keen spirit of discretion. Her corrections to the Constitutions of Hugolino are all of this kind. For example, take the prescriptions about enclosure. The Constitutions of Hugolino prescribe that the nuns

> . . . remain enclosed the whole time of their life. After they have entered the enclosure of this religion and have assumed the religious habit, they should never be granted any permission or faculty to leave this enclosure, unless perhaps some are transferred to another place to plant or build up this same religion. Moreover it is fitting that, when they die, both ladies as well as servants who are professed should be buried within the enclosure.[178]

The corresponding passage in Clare also considers that after the newly professed have put on the habit, 'she may not go outside the monastery' and immediately adds 'except for a useful, reasonable, evident and justifiable purpose.'[179]

In the same way, with regard to silence, Hugolino anticipated

Let a continuous silence be kept by all at all times, so that it is not allowed either for one to talk to another or for another to talk to her without permission, except for those on whom some teaching office or duty had been enjoined, which cannot fittingly be discharged in silence.[180]

Clare says, 'let the sisters keep silence' and then adds 'from the hour of Compline until Terce' which means during the night—very understandable in a community where they slept fifty in a single dormitory. She also provided for exceptions in the infirmary where one may always speak during the night:

At all times, however, they may be permitted to speak with discernment in the infirmary for the recreation and service of the sick.

These are small differences and it is quite clear from the examples that Clare too appreciated the value of silence. However she adds:

The sisters may, always and everywhere, communicate what is necessary, briefly and in a quiet voice.[181]

These small differences, however, make a great deal of difference. Where Hugolino is always anxious to prevent any possibility of abuse or relaxation, Clare puts her trust in her sisters in the conviction, which is always implicit in her Rule, that those who have chosen to live at San Damiano are doing so willingly.

The Rule of Clare was approved, as has been said, only two days before her death. Innocent IV, en route through Assisi, went to visit San Damiano and was struck by the holiness of Clare. For sure, it was only this extraordinary circumstance that brought about the approval of the first rule of religious life for women written by a woman, or anyway the first of whom we have any mention in the history of the Church.

For whom was this Rule written? For San Damiano, certainly, but also for other monasteries. Very soon afterwards, Agnes of Bohemia was successful in obtaining it for her community in Prague. The choice of the Rule of St Clare did not mean that the community left the Order of San Damiano but only that this was their particular approach within that Order.

Ten years later, in 1263, Urban IV wanted to bring to an end the juridical confusion which characterised the Damianite communities, and he wrote another Rule for them changing the name of the Order yet again, so that from then on it would be known as the Order of Saint Clare. Urban referred back primarily to the Constitutions of Hugolino, inserting the changes of the Rule of Innocent IV in the matter of property but removing any explicit reference to Clare's own Rule. In particular the introduction to his Rule runs like this:

> For all those who, abandoning the vanities of the world, want to embrace your Religion and to live in it, it is suitable, indeed necessary, that they observe these laws of life and discipline, living in obedience, without anything of their own and in chastity, in enclosure.[182]

There is no reference here to Francis as the founder of the Order, nor any indication of the Gospel as the heart of the sisters' life, which Clare had taken from the *Regula bullata*. Only in a few instances, as when he requires that the abbess listen equally to all the community before admitting a new sister, does the Rule of Urban IV refer to the Rule of Clare, but still without actually quoting her.

At this point we find ourselves back where we began, asking: who founded the Poor Clares? If we read the first words of the Rule of Clare, the answer is clear:

> The Form of Life of the Order of the Poor Sisters, which blessed Francis established, is this: to observe the holy Gospel of our Lord

Jesus Christ, by living in obedience, without anything of one's own, and in chastity.[183]

According to Clare, the founder was Francis.

Gregory IX, too, in a letter to Agnes of Bohemia in 1238, declared that Francis:

> ...brought a grand increase of souls to the Son of the Eternal Father when he instituted Three orders throughout the breadth of the world, in which during every single day the All Powerful is rendered glorious in many ways.[184]

These three Orders, according to the testimony of Gregory, are the Order of Friars Minor, Lesser Brother, the cloistered Sisters and the communities of Penitents.[185] This is the first official document in which Francis is indicated as the founder of the three Orders. So— there seems to be no problem. The founder of the second Franciscan Order is Francis. However, as we have seen, Gregory had an big investment in taking over the spiritual fatherhood of the Order of San Damiano even from Francis himself, since by so doing, he was able to confer on both the order founded by himself and the rule attributed to him 'a spiritual authority' which was beyond dispute. On the other hand, Clare certainly maintained it was Francis, right to the end of her life, when the umbrella of the universally venerated Francis had helped obtain approval for a rule which had, in fact, been written by a woman.

Another hypothesis is that the foundress of the Second Order is Clare herself. It has been noted that

> the traditional position of Franciscan history—at least within the Order—is now superseded, that position according to which Clare would be seen as the foundress of the second Franciscan Order, or, at least, of the Order of Poor Clares which is a definition that,

strictly speaking, cannot possibly be applied to the Damianite monasteries until after the promulgation of the Urbanite Rule in 1263.[186]

The third hypothesis is that the founder of the second order would have been Cardinal Hugolino himself. This third theory absolutely cannot be considered with regard to the particular community at San Damiano.

The most convincing theory, given the present state of studies, is that the Order which took the name of St Clare from 1263 had two founders: Clare and Hugolino. Both of them, in fact, not only promoted the actual establishment of various religious communities, but both of them also wrote an approved juridical text which regulated the way of life within those communities. Both of them can be considered to all extents and purposes to have been the founders. This means that right from the start there were two spirits at work within the Order: that which came from the lady of Assisi and that which came from the cardinal who later became pope.

In the course of the following centuries, the majority of the Poor Clare communities followed the rule of Urban IV which closely followed the arrangements of the Constitutions of Hugolino. A small group of monasteries, however, has always continued to follow the Rule of Clare. Especially at times of reform within the Order, for instance that of the Observants and again under the influence of Saint Colette, the Poor Clares have always chosen to return to the Rule of Clare, and this was especially so in the second half of the twentieth century, when the Vatican Council invited all religious to recover the charism of their founders. At that point, the large majority of Clares felt free to choose to return to the Rule of Clare. Thus it is only in these most recent years that the Order of Saint Clare has come to have one sole spirit: that of its foundress, Clare of Assisi.

· · · · · · · · · ·

CHAPTER
NINE

WAR AND PEACE

The beginning of the thirteenth
century in the Italian peninsula was characterised by a situation of
great political instability. The opposition between the two massive
medieval powers of the emperor and the papacy marked these years
with a particular violence. Such an opposition affected all the struc-
tures of society: the great feudal laity and ecclesiastics and also the
new city institutions which, during these years, were establishing the
Communes.

In fact the Italian cities which during the conflict with Barbarossa
in the preceding century, had affirmed their political and military
autonomy for the first time, were still deeply divided within themselves. At the beginning of the century, the governing group was still
drawn from the *boni homines*, the good men, which meant the aristocracy. These, far from renouncing their traditional power base in the
cities, were definitely well entrenched and building fortified houses
even within the city walls. Side by side with them another social
group was emerging with increasing importance, a group composed
of the merchants, officials and even functionaries from the episcopal
curia. In the sources, these last were all called the *homines populi*, men
of the people. The whole history of the first half of the thirteenth

century was marked by the conflict between the *boni homines,* also called *maiores,* and the *homines populi* or *minores.* The *minores* made up the bulk of the city's army and were mainly *pedites,* foot soldiers, while the *boni homines* represented the ancient and traditional warfare of aristocratic origin and they came to be known as *milites* or knights.

To this extent, the situation of Assisi was typical. The conflict between the *boni homines (maiores)* and the *homines populi (minores)* came to a head in 1198 when the *minores* rebelled against the imperial troops stationed in the Rocca and against the *boni homines* who were their allies. Assisi as an imperial city came to an end during those years. Frederick Barbarossa had granted them a charter in 1160 by which the city came under his direct authority. From 1177 there are records of the presence in the city of Conrad of Urslingen, an imperial functionary holding the titles of Duke of Spoleto and Count of Assisi. It is possible that during these years the emperor himself had stayed in the city several times. In 1198, indeed, a few months after the death of Henry VI who was the son Barbarossa expected to succeed him on the imperial throne, the *minores* took advantage of a difficult political moment for Conrad of Urslingen and attacked the Rocca, thus taking command of the city. A number of *maiores* decided to abandon the city and seek refuge in nearby Perugia. Among those who chose this path of exile was the family of Favarone di Offreduccio, the father of Clare. In Perugia, these families were welcomed by the *boni homines* of the city. The sources for the life of Clare say nothing about these years spent outside the city because of the war. We know that some of Clare's first companions at San Damiano came from Perugia, a sure sign that during those years Clare knew how to form lasting friendships and how to remain in contact with those friends after her return to Assisi. The conditions of the flight to Perugia would not of themselves have been particularly severe although at the same time we must not underestimate that fact that Clare, as a small girl, knew the impact of war.

This option of the *boni homines* simply extended the conflict. What had been an internal struggle within the city of Assisi developed into war between the Communes. Perugia allied herself with the refugees who had taken shelter there and went to war against their city neighbour. In 1202 at Collestrada, halfway between Assisi and Perugia, a battle took place at which the Assisi troops were defeated. This enabled an agreement which formed the basis of a peace treaty and as a result the aristocratic families of Assisi returned to the town somewhere between 1203 and 1210. A Peace Charter was signed by the contenders in 1203 which enables us better to identify the families that made up the *maiores*. This was a nucleus of about twenty families, all of aristocratic lineage, all having their houses in the upper part of the city beneath the Rocca or near the church of San Rufino and who continued in possession of the government of the district.

The culture of this aristocratic group was, as we have said, deeply dyed with the values of warfare. Knighthood meant the art of war, sung by the jongleurs and troubadours. Spring was the season for war, the end of the rain permitting knights and horses once again to set forth. This is the 'lovely May' sung about by Bertran de Born:

> The bright season of spring rejoices my heart—
> that season when leaves and flowers come forth,
> and I am happy when I hear the fiesta of the birds
> who make their songs resound through the woods,
> I am happy when I see
> awnings and pavilions
> set up on the grass;
> I know great joy
> when across the land I see
> knights and horses armed for war.[187]

Despite the joyful tone of this verse, however, war was no picnic even in the thirteenth century. It is true that the number of knights was often very small and that the offensive weapons were not very sophisticated, but it is also true that the chronicles are full of horror stories and the suffering which every war brings with its sad train of famine and epidemic. Even graver was the situation in which, as has been observed,

> the struggle for power was unrelenting; the vendetta was a custom which was considered simultaneously a privilege and a right/obligation of the aristocracy who were the ones bearing arms and who lived a kind of courtly life. This vendetta imposed on the streets and piazze of the cities a climate of more or less endemic civil war.[188]

You could describe war in thirteenth century Italy as a series of concentric circles. In the first circle would be civil war within the city between the different groups of families, primarily for dominance and later between the *maiores* and the *minores*. The entire century was marked by this hard social confrontation, in the course of which the 'people's party' progressively increased its own power.

This first level of conflict is closely connected with the second: that between different cities. Here too the story of Assisi is an example: just as the conflict between *maiores* and *minores* in the Umbrian city led to war with neighbouring Perugia, so all too often the political growth of the other Communes of central and north Italy was accompanied by conflict with their neighbouring cities for control of the district. Every city, in fact, found its strength and its *raison d'etre* in trade, which became the centre of a whole network of an economic system. The surrounding countryside was essential as a source of produce and manpower to feed the citizens of the economic area. From this arose the thrust of the authorities of the city to free themselves from every feudal-style power and to strengthen the central control of an ever-expanding territory. As a result, the interests of each city were in conflict with those of the neighbouring cities and this in turn led to a never-ending state of war and rivalry.

During the course of the century, this internal strife within the cities and between the cities gradually assumed a mature political connotation, with the various groups giving allegiance to one or other of the two great alliances which all this time were carving up the peninsula between them. So we begin to say that every city was divided between Guelph or Ghibelline, the first being supporters of the pope and the second of the emperor. This was the third level of war in the thirteenth century, that of the conflict between these two great powers of Christendom, pope and emperor.

The struggle between Frederick II and Gregory IX was as intense as it was bitter and in the end it involved everything and everyone. However, this was not the highest level of war in the thirteenth century. The fourth and highest level was that of the conflict between Christianity and Islam, the Crusades. When he received the imperial crown, Frederick II promised to go on crusade. It was because of this unfulfilled promise that he was excommunicated for the first time by the pope.

These four levels of war in the thirteenth century were all interconnected among themselves. The crusades were the cause of litigation and then of open warfare between pope and emperor. The struggle between these two was in turn the source of the division of the Italian cities into Guelph and Ghibelline and this was what might be called the ideological packaging of the internal strife of the cities. The plot of the different forms of war was not only political. From the beginning of the thirteenth century, after Saladin had recaptured

Jerusalem in 1187, the thrust of the crusades was not without its delusions. The consequences of that long century of conflict took a long time to burn themselves out. Even though it is not easy, from a historian's point of view, to weigh up such a complex phenomenon, yet we can certainly echo the words of Jacques le Goff:

> that the crusades had contributed to the impoverishment of the West, and in particular to the impoverishment of the knightly classes, and at the same time as creating a moral unity of Christendom they also contributed to a sharpening up of the nascent national contrasts; that the crusades had opened up a definitive breach between the West and the Byzantine, and that, along with changes of habit and custom, the holy war led the crusaders into the worst excesses of the pogroms perpetrated on their journey and to massacres and sacrileges. [...] Finally, the military orders, powerless to defend and keep the Holy Land, had to retreat to the West where they abandoned themselves to every kind of financial and military exaction. All this was the passive burden of the project.[189]

One particular consequence continued to produce its fruit of blood in the time of Clare and Francis of Assisi, and this was the growth and spread of intolerance. Every war produces its culture of hostility and the fallout lasts beyond the close of military hostilities. The people who took part in the first wave of the crusades never reached the Muslim heretic across the sea, but along the way they encountered Jews who had lived for centuries in western Europe. Hatred demanded an enemy and often created its own, finding it even among the most innocent. This is the root of the anti-Jewish pogrom of 1096 and the years which followed. According to the testimony of Albert of Aix:

they broke the locks and forced the doors, they sought out and killed seven hundred who vainly tried to defend themselves against this far superior force. [...] Only a small number of Jews escaped this cruel massacre and some accepted baptism, far more out of fear than for love of the Christian faith.[190]

To some extent it is possible to trace the arc of the development and growth of this culture of intolerance right through the twelfth century, from opposition to the Muslims to the persecution of all who were perceived as different, or as heretics and schismatics. Amid all these feelings of opposition, there was one which is particularly striking because of the fragility of those who were its object—that is, the hostility towards lepers. Even leprosy was a fruit of the crusades. It is not that there were no contagious diseases of the skin in the West before the beginning of the eleventh century, only that the number of the sick had been more or less contained. The real spread of leprosy followed the return of the crusaders from across the sea.

Confronted with leprosy, the attitudes of the western Christians were more or less unanimous. The basic principle was the sanction set out in the book of Leviticus:

Anyone who is discovered to have leprosy must tear his clothes and let his hair grow in wild disarray, and cover his upper lip and call out as he goes: I am a leper, I am a leper. As long as the disease lasts he is defiled and must live outside the camp.[191]

From the time of the third Lateran Council in 1179, leprosaria had multiplied across the whole of Europe. Certainly there were occasions when many men and women showed compassion towards these afflicted people, but on the whole the principle was one of the exclusion and then the confining of those who were considered to be a danger. The exclusion was all the stronger because it was thought that leprosy was transmitted through sexual contact, so the afflicted were twice cursed because they were seen as suffering the consequences of their sins. Even the courtly literature contributed towards creating this prejudice, as in the terrible story of Béroul, in which King Mark consigns Isotta (Isolde) to the leper colony:

> One hundred deformed lepers, the flesh of their faces disfigured and discoloured, hurried up on their crutches with a thumping of sticks and gathered near the stake and, under their swollen eyelids, their bloodshot eyes rejoiced at the spectacle. Yvain, the most terrible of the sick men, shouted out to the king in a shrill voice: Sire, throw your wife into these arms, it would be good justice though far too short. This great flame will swiftly burn her up, this strong wind will soon scatter her ashes. And when this flame will, in a short time, have died down, your punishment of her will be over. If you want, I could teach you a far worse punishment so that she will live on in great dishonour, always longing for death? Would you like that, O King?
>
> And the king replied: yes, that she live on but in great dishonour and a condition worse than death. If anyone could teach me such a torture, I would be grateful to him.
>
> Sire, I will tell you my idea briefly. See, I have twenty companions here. Give us Isotta so that she belongs to us all! Our illness increases our desires. Give her to your lepers. No woman ever had a worse fate. See how we are glued together by our tears. She, at your side, delighted in rich fabrics lined with jewels, with rooms decorated in marble, who with you tasted sweet wine and enjoyed honours and joys, when she sees the court of the lepers, when she enters our huts and lies down with us, Isotta the beautiful, Isotta the Fair, will really know her sin and will weep all over again for this beautiful fire of brambles!

The king listened, then he stood up and remained motionless for a long time. Then he ran towards the queen and took her hand. She cried: Have pity, Sire, send me to the flames instead, send me to the flames!

The king thrust her away, Yvain took her and a hundred sick men gathered around her. Hearing them shouting and squeaking, every heart was moved with pity, but Yvain was joyful. Isotta had come, Yvain led her away with him. Out of the city went the repugnant procession.[192]

It was not chance therefore that the instinct for peace of Francis of Assisi should mature into an option of mercy towards the lepers. In his Testament, he opens with the words:

The Lord gave me, Brother Francis, thus to begin doing penance in this way: for when I was in sin, it seemed too bitter for me to see lepers. And the Lord himself led me among them and I showed mercy to them.

Then he goes on to say:

And the Lord revealed a greeting to me, that we should say: May the Lord give you peace.[193]

Francis' option for peace arose from his compassion for the victim. According to the beautiful testimony of his companions, he compared his search for peace with healing for the sick:

As you announce peace with your mouth, make sure that greater peace is in your hearts. Let no-one be provoked to anger or scandal through you, but may everyone be drawn to peace, kindness and harmony through your gentleness. For we have been called to this: to heal the wounded, bind up the broken and recall the erring.[194]

Francis made peace the heart of his teaching:

> In all of his preaching, before he presented the Word of God to the
> assembly, he prayed for peace, saying: May the Lord give you
> peace![195]

This preaching rapidly became a definite task in the face of the wars
between the Italian cities. In Perugia he warned them to fear civil
war because of the pride and injustice of the city's nobility.[196] At
Arezzo he and his companion Brother Sylvester urged them to pray
against the demon of war which was devastating the city.[197] At
Bologna, according to Thomas of Spoleto, he preached about angels,
men and demons, inviting the inhabitants of that city to cast out
hatred and to draw up a new peace treaty, and the evidence confirms
that on this occasion many noble families who had been divided by
hatred, were reconciled among themselves.

Francis showed himself well aware that war is born in the human
heart and that therefore the first victory to be sought is victory over
every form of hatred and resentment. This evangelical meekness, to
which is promised the inheritance of the earth, is not by any means
a form of disembodied spiritualism. Francis did not disdain to enter
into the heart of the contradictions of his time in order to seek peace
of heart, but without despising the more concrete method of political agreement.

It is possible to trace Francis' actions for peace in a way which contradicts the concentric circles of war we spoke about earlier.
Beginning with the lepers, that is with the victims of intolerance,
Francis was less interested in the conflicts which were churning up
the Italian cities, but he did not neglect to direct words of peace to
the pope and the emperor. When he was speaking about peace,
Francis seems to have found a particularly authoritative tone, as in

that beautiful discourse which, according to the so-called *Legend of Perugia* he would have wanted to say to the emperor:

> If I had a chance to speak to the emperor , I would beg him, for the love of God, and I would ask him to issue an edict that on Christmas Day the poor would be amply provided for by the well-off. [198]

The high point of Francis' longing for peace is shown in his famous dialogue with the Sultan of Egypt, to whom he presented himself unarmed and accompanied only by a single brother. The chronicles of the Fifth Crusade reveal how disconcerting was this initiative on the part of a man almost unknown. The incident has impressed everyone beginning with Giotto and Dante and there is no need to dwell on it here. It is enough to underline the strong bond which unites the option of mercy for the lepers and the dialogue with the Sultan. In both cases Francis knew how to overcome the limitations of prejudice by going to speak with the excluded and with the enemy.

And Clare? How did the lady of Assisi share in Francis' dream of peace? She would not have been insensitive to his preaching of peace, coming as she did from a family of knights, impregnated by the culture of war, and as a young girl having had some experience of exile. The sources say that from her youth she was 'of a very good life and that she was intent upon and occupied with works of piety'. [199] There are no explicit references to Clare working with the lepers and it is possible that towards them her piety expressed itself in an indirect way, even while she was in her father's house. Afterwards, however, when she had made her option at St Mary of the Porziuncola to follow as a poor woman the poor Christ, Clare shared in Francis' vision of peace.

For both Francis and Clare, renunciation of all forms of the exercise of power did not include an option for impotence in the face of evil. Gospel meekness does not mean being disarmed, although its armaments are not the same as those which wage war. The first episode in Clare's life when she was obliged to measure herself against the arrogance of the violent, was that of the liberation of her sister Agnes from the hands of their relatives.

Sixteen days after the conversion of Clare, Agnes—inspired by the divine spirit—ran to her sister, revealed the secret of her will and told her that she wished to serve God completely. Embracing her with joy, Clare said: I thank God, most sweet sister, that he has heard my concern for you.

A no less marvellous defence followed this conversion. For while the joyful sisters were clinging to the footprints of Christ in the church of Sant'Angelo in Panzo, and she who had heard more from the Lord was teaching her novice sister, new attacks by relatives were quickly flaring up against the young girls.

> The next day, hearing that Agnes had gone off to Clare, twelve men burning with anger and hiding outwardly their evil intent, ran to the place [and] pretended to make a peaceful entrance. Immediately they turned to Agnes, since they had long ago lost hope of Clare, and said: Why have you come to this place? Get ready to return with us immediately.
>
> When she responded that she did not want to leave her sister Clare, one of the knights in a fierce mood ran towards her and without sparing blows and kicks, tried to drag her away by her hair, while the others pushed her and lifted her up in their arms. At this, as if she had been captured by lions and been torn from the Lord, the young girl cried out: Dear sister, help me! Do not let me be taken from Christ the Lord! While the violent robbers were

dragging the young girl along the slope of the mountain, ripping her clothes and strewing the path with the hair they had torn out, Clare prostrated herself in prayer with tears, begged that her sister would be given constancy of mind and that the strength of humans would be overcome by divine power.

Suddenly, in fact, Agnes's body lying on the ground seemed so heavy that the men, many as there were, exerted all their energy and were not able to carry her beyond a certain stream. Even others, running from their fields and vineyards, attempted to give them some help, but they could in no way lift that body from the earth. When they failed they shrugged off the miracle by mocking: She has been eating lead all night, no wonder she is so heavy.

Then Lord Monaldo, her enraged uncle, intended to strike her a lethal blow, but an awful pain suddenly struck the hand he raised and for a long time the anguish of pain afflicted it.[200]

The weapon with which Clare responded to violence was that of prayer—and what an efficacious weapon, too. The fist which their uncle Monaldo—almost mad with anger—raised to strike Agnes was, in all probability, an ironclad fist and his action capable of killing Agnes. Clare's prayer froze her uncle's arm in the middle of his violent gesture and saved her sister who was free from that moment to follow her own path.

Clare continued to accompany Francis in his Gospel dream, even when this was stretched out across the whole world. While she lived always at San Damiano, she did not feel herself to have no part in things that happened far from Assisi. According to the evidence collected from some of the sisters at the canonisation process

The lady Clare had such a fervent spirit she willingly wanted to endure martyrdom for love of the Lord. She showed this when, after she had heard certain brothers had been martyred in Morocco, she said she wanted to go there. Then, because of this, the witness wept. This was before she was so sick.[201]

This evidence is all the more notable in that her biographer did not consider it suitable to be included in the official biography, a clear sign that it was not considered appropriate to propagate the idea that an abbess of a cloistered monastery might abandon everything and go to Morocco. Sister Cecilia who tells us this episode, took Clare's intention very seriously, enough to burst into tears over it. The fact she is referring to is undoubtedly the martyrdom of the first Franciscan friars in Morocco in 1220.

This participation in the Franciscan task of peace showed itself again later and reveals exactly this point of the extent to which Clare was in tune with the spirit and actions of Francis. Among all the 'peace initiatives' realised by Francis, the most notable was certainly that of the reconciliation between the bishop and the podestà of Assisi. This came about when the saint was already very ill. Let us listen to the account of the *Legend of Perugia*:

> At the time when he was very sick—the Praises of the Lord had already been composed—the bishop of Assisi excommunicated the podestà. In return, the podestà had it announced to the sound of the trumpet in the streets of the city that every citizen was forbidden to buy from or sell anything whatsoever to the bishop or to transact any business with him. There was a savage hatred between them. Blessed Francis, who was very sick at that time, pitied them. It pained him to see that no-one, religious or lay, intervened to re-establish peace and concord between them. So he said to his companions: It is a great shame for us, the servants of God, that at a time when the podestà and bishop so hate each

other, no-one can be found to re-establish peace and concord between them! On this occasion he added the following strophe to his canticle:

All praise be you, my Lord,

through those who grant pardon for love of you;

through those who endure sickness and trial.

Happy those who endure in peace;

by you, Most High, they will be crowned.

He then called one of his companions and said to him: 'Go and find the podestà and tell him from me that he should go to the bishop's palace with the notables of the commune and with all those he can assemble'. When the brother had left, he said to the others: 'Go and in the presence of the bishop, of the podestà and of the entire gathering, sing the Canticle of Brother Sun. I have confidence that the Lord will put humility and peace in their hearts and that they will return to their former friendship and affection.'

When everyone had gathered at the place of the cloister of the bishop's palace, the two brothers stood up and one of them was the spokesman: 'Despite his sufferings, blessed Francis' he said, 'has composed the 'Praises of the Lord' for all his creatures, to the praise of God and for the edification of his neighbour; he asks you to listen with great devotion.'

With that, they began to sing. The podestà stood up and joined his hands as for the gospel of the Lord, and he listened with great recollection and attention; soon tears flowed from his eyes, for he had a great deal of confidence in blessed Francis and devotion for him. At the end of the canticle, the podestà cried out before the entire gathering: 'In truth, I say to you, not only do I forgive the lord bishop whom I ought to recognise as my master, but I would even pardon my brother's and my son's murderer!' He then threw himself at the feet of the lord bishop and said to him: 'For the love of our Lord Jesus Christ and of blessed Francis his servant, I am ready to make any atonement you wish.' The bishop stood up and said to him: 'My office demands humility of me, but by nature I am quick to anger; you must forgive me!' With much tenderness and affection, they both locked arms and embraced each other.[202]

There is an exact parallel to this in the life of Clare, told us in the *Legend of St Clare the Virgin*:

Another time, Vitalis d'Aversa, captain of an imperial army, a man craving glory and bold in battle, directed that army against Assisi. He stripped the land of trees, devastated the entire countryside and so settled down to besiege the city. He declared with threatening words that he would in no way withdraw until he had taken possession of that city. It had already come to the point that danger to the city was feared imminent. When Clare, the servant of Christ, heard this, she was profoundly grieved, called the sisters around her and said: Dearest children, every day we receive many good things from that city. It would be terrible if at a proper time, we did not help it, as we now can. She commanded that some ashes be brought and that the sisters bare their heads. First she scattered a lot of ashes over her own head, and then placed them on the heads of those sisters. 'Go to our Lord' she said, 'and with all your heart beg for the liberation of the city'.

Why should I narrate the details? Why describe again the tears of the virgins, their impassioned prayers? On the following morning, the merciful God brought about a happy ending to the trial so that, after the entire army had been dispersed, the proud man departed contrary to his vow and never again disturbed that land.[203]

For both Francis and Clare, the point of departure was their sense of shame that they found nobody working to promote peace. Both felt themselves responsible. But confronted with war, what exactly was their responsibility? In the face of hatred, the instinctive reaction is to believe oneself impotent and therefore justified in inertia. Instead, both Francis and Clare felt the responsibility of giving some reaction. This sense of responsibility is all the more striking when we recall the extreme weakness of them both at that time: Francis because he was ill, blind and unable to move; Clare because she was a woman and without power through of her choice to live cloistered at San Damiano. What could either of them do? They could turn to God in prayer and the *Praises* of Francis are in fact a prayer. Both Francis and Clare invented (so to speak) a liturgy. That of Francis is a liturgy of praise into which both bishop and podestà were drawn (with great devotion, as people who read the Gospel). For Clare and her sisters at San Damiano, theirs was a liturgy of penitence, sprinkling ashes on each others' heads. The general sense is the same: prayer overcomes war, scatters hatred, distances us from violence. God loves peace and those who wage war must therefore be distanced from the mind of God. It is the task of one who seeks peace to call on God to turn again and be once more present to the human conscience. The power of prayer is the true weapon of the weak.

Her awareness of this weak power of prayer comes out very clearly in another episode of Clare's life.

> The Spoleto valley more often drank of the chalice of wrath because of that scourge the Church had to endure in various parts of the world under Frederick the Emperor. In it there was a battle array of soldiers and Saracen archers swarming like bees at the imperial command to depopulate its villages and to spoil its cities. Once when the fury of the enemy pressed upon Assisi, a city dear

to the Lord, and the army was already near its gates, the Saracens, worst of people, who thirsted for the blood of Christians and attempted imprudently every outrage, rushed upon San Damiano, entered the confines of the place and even the enclosure of the virgins. The hearts of the ladies melted with fear; their voices trembled with it, and they brought their tears to their mother. She, with an undaunted heart, ordered that she be brought, sick as she was, to the door and placed there before the enemy, while the silver pyx enclosed in ivory in which the Body of the Holy of Holies was most devotedly reserved, preceded her.

When she had thoroughly prostrated herself to the Lord in prayer, she said to her Christ with tears: 'Look, my Lord, do you wish to deliver into the hands of pagans your defenceless servants whom you have nourished with your own love? Lord, I beg you, defend these your servants whom I am not able to defend at this time'

Suddenly a voice from the mercy seat of new grace, as if of a little child, resounded in her ears: 'I will always defend you'.

'My Lord,' she said, 'please protect this city which for your love sustains us'.

And the Lord said to her: It will suffer afflictions but will be defended by my protection.

Then the virgin, raising her tear-filled face, comforted the weeping sisters, saying: 'My dear children, I guarantee you will not suffer any harm. Just have confidence in Christ'.

Without delay, the subdued boldness of those dogs began immediately to be alarmed. They were driven away by the power of the one who was praying, departing in haste over those walls which they had scaled.

Immediately Clare advised those who had heard the voice mentioned above, saying eagerly to them: Dearest children, be careful not to reveal in any way that voice to anyone while I am still in the body.[204]

Here we have all the protagonists of thirteenth century war: the excommunicated emperor Frederick II and the Saracens of his imperial army. It has already been mentioned that Frederick, who was king of Sicily, found many Arabs on the island who had been there when he first took power. The emperor organised their transfer to Puglia and at the same time shaped them into his elite troops. The author of the *Legend* presents them as 'thirsting for Christian blood' and thus makes this episode into a continuation of the spirit of the crusades. This moment could certainly be called the moment in Clare's life when she was at her weakest. On other occasions, she had had to confront poverty and even penury but now she had to confront not only illness and her own death but also the deaths of her sisters.

In this extremity of poverty, Clare turned to God, sending a prayer which was almost a wail. In her evidence at the canonisation process, Sr Francesca is much drier: 'Lord, look upon these servants of yours because I cannot protect them.'[205] It is the cry of one who no longer has any power and therefore trusts in God.

Here too we find a liturgy: Clare prays before the Blessed Sacrament and, after her prayer, is confident that she has been heard and turns at once to her sisters to comfort them saying: My sisters and daughters place me before them.[206] The author of the *Legend* notes that the Saracens 'hurried away, overcome by the power of prayer.' It is easy to imagine that the Saracens were actually less bestial than the *Legend* presents them and—as was the Muslim custom— that they would have been brought to a halt by a community of women at prayer. In any case, the incident is recounted a number of times in the Acts of the Canonisation Process as an example of the power of Clare's prayers at this moment of her greatest weakness. This is the true alternative to war. Clare, like Francis, was not paralysed by her sense of powerlessness but rather, entrusting herself to prayer, she built an actual approach to peace.

NOTES

SIGNS AND ABBREVIATIONS

1. ★ – to be found in *Clare of Assisi: Early Documents, The Lady.*

INTRODUCTION

2. 1 Cel 20 Omnibus Vol 1, pp. 198–199.
3. Jacques Le Goff, *San Luigi,* Turin 1996, Part 2.
4. Cf J. Delarun, *The Misadventure of Francis of Assisi.*

CHAPTER ONE

5. 1 Cel 18RegnBull.
6. 1 Cel 20.
7. While we remember the extraordinary cultus of Anthony of Padua, we also recall that this cult arose after his death.
8. *LegCl* 14; *Proc* I, 13; II, 22; III, 14.
9. *Proc* VI, 6.
10. This phrase 'Povere dame recluse' has become almost a technical term. I have translated it rather clumsily with a comma as being the most manageable way in English (translator).
11. Called 'The Remembrance of the Desires of a Soul' in the *Omnibus of Sources.*
12. *AFH* 54 (1961) pp. 3–25.
13. *LegCl* 37.
14. *2Ag* 10–14.
15. *2Ag* 15–18.
16. For this whole question, see Giulia Barone: *Da frate Elia agli spirituali,* Milan 1999.
17. 2 Cel 204.
18. *RegCl* 6, 2–5.
19. Ubertino da Casale: *The Tree of the Crucified Life of Jesus.*

CHAPTER TWO

20. *LegCl* 47.

21. *Ibid.*

22. Cf Z. Lazzeri, AFH 13 (1920) p. 496, *CA:ED*, 1993 p. 129.

23. Notification of Death *CA:ED*, p. 137.

24. *Ibid CA:ED*, p. 138.

25. *Gloriosus Deus*, 18 October 1253, BF I, pp. 684–685.

26. Florence, Biblioteca Nazionale, cod. Finaly–Landau 251. This codex, which was the property of a certain abbess of Santa Chiara Novella in Florence, one Cherubina Deborgianni, also contains the Life of Clare by Ugolino da Verino, the Rule of Clare (in Latin), and her Testament with the Blessing (in an Italian translation), as well as a number of other works. It is thanks to the initiative of this woman religious from the sixteenth century that the Acts of Clare's canonisation process were preserved at all, even though only in a translation made in the previous century.

27. The bull of Innocent IV marking the break with the Friars is *Etsi animarum* (22 October 1254) BF II, pp. 259–261.

28. Alexander IV, *Nec insolitum* (22 December 1254) in BF II, pp. 261–262.

29. S. Brufani, *La Bulla Canonizationis di Chiara d'Assisi*, in Fontes Francescani, pp. 281–283.

30. G. La Grasta, *La canizazzione diChiara*, cit., p. 318.

31. Alexander IV, *Clare claris praeclara*, 4 in AFH 13 (1920) Appendix p. 502 and *CA:ED*, p. 240.

32. F. Pennacchi, *Legenda sanctae Clarae virginis*, Assisi 1910, p. xx.

33. Published in Z. Lazzeri, *La vita di santa Chiara, raccolta e tradotta da tutte le fonti conosciute e completata col testo inedito del Processo si canonizazzione per un francescano toscano del Cinquecento.*

34. *LegCl* Preface: *CA:ED*, p. 251.

35. This reference to the 'companions of Francis', is particularly interesting in that it must refer to Leo and those who spoke about Francis' life (especially the last two years) with particular intimacy, and in 1255–56 when the *Legend* was being written, their witness bore great authority.

36. *LegCl* Preface: *CA:ED*, p. 277.

37. *LegCl* Preface *CA:ED*, p 278.

38. S. Brufani, *Le 'legendae' agigrafiche di Chiara d'Assisi*, in *Chiara d'Assisi*, cit. p. 355.

39. The full text of Clare's writings is to be found in *Clare of Assisi: Early Documents, The Lady.*

CHAPTER THREE

40. *CanProc* XX, 1–3.

41. *CanProc* XX, 3.

42. *CanProc* XIX, 1.

43. G. Duby, *L'arte e la società medievale*, Rome–Bari 1977, p. 49.

44. J. Le Goff, *Società tripartite, ideologia monarchia e rinnovamento economico nella cristianità dal secolo IX ak XII*, in Id., *Tempo della Chiesa e tempo del mercante e altri saggi sul lavoro e la cultura nel Medioevo*, Turin 1977, p. 41.

45. G. Duby, *Le origine dell'economia europea* Bari 1975, p. 212.

46. G. Duby, *L'arte e la società medievale*, cit., pp. 154–155.

47. Regine Pernoud, *La donna al tempo delle cattedrali*, Milan 1982, p. 101.

48. G. Duby, *L'arte e la società medievale*, cit. pp 49–50.

49. Cit in G. Macchia: *La letteratura francese nel Medievo*, Turin 1973, p. 158.

50. *CanProc* XIII, 2.

51. *CanProc* I, 1.

52. *CanProc* XVII, 4.

53. Dante, *Vita Nuova* XXVI.

54. *CanProc* II, 2.

55. *CanProc* XVI, 2.

56. *CanProc* XIX, 2.

57. *CanProc* XVIII, 2.

58. *CanProc* XVIII, 2.

CHAPTER FOUR

59. Test Francis 1–4.

60. Athanasius, *Vita Antonii*, nn. 2–3 PG 26, 835–897.

61. John 3, 5.

62. 1 Cel 2.

63. 1 Cel 3–4.

64. Mk 1, 15.

65. cf Mt 3, 2.
66. cf John 17, 15–16.
67. 1 Cel 103.
68. *CanProc* XII, 2–4.
69. *Clara claris praeclara* nn. 6–8.
70. *LegCl* 5.
71. *CanProc* XVII, 2–3.
72. *CanProc* XVII, 7.
73. *RegCl* 6.1.
74. *LegCl* 5.
75. *LegCl* 6; *CanProc* I, 2; III, 1; IV, 2;VI, 1; XII, 2; XVI, 3, 6; XX, 6.
76. *CanProc* XVII, 5.
77. *LegCl* 7–8; *CanProc* x, 4; XVI, 6; XVII, 5; XVIII, 3; XX, 6.
78. P. Sabatier, *Vie de saint François d'Assise* Paris 1926, p. 173.
79. L. Padovese, *La tonsura di Chiara* in *Chiara, francescanesimo al femminile* ed. D. Covi and D. Dozzi, Rome 1992, pp. 393–406.
80. RnB XII, 3.
81. *LegCl* 8.
82. *Clara claris praeclara* 8.
83. *LegCl* 9.
84. *Clara claris praeclara* 7, 8.
85. *CanProc* XII, 3.
86. *CanProc* XIII, 1.
87. *LegPer* 111.
88. *LegPer* 52.

CHAPTER FIVE

89. Cf *CanProc* XII, 5; *LegCl* 10.
90. Previously called Catherine, cf *Chronicle of the XXIV Generals*. AFH III, p. 175.
91. *LegCl* 24.
92. *Ibid.*
93. *Ibid.*
94. *LegCl* 25.
95. *LegCl* 26.

96. *LegCl* 10.
97. I. Magli, *Gli uomini della penitenza* Milan 1977, p. 47.
98. *RegCl* 6, 1–5.
99. *RnB* XII, 3.
100. *TestCl* 24.
101. I. Magli, *Gli uomini della penitenza,* cit., p. 38.
102. Letter of Jacques de Vitry, *CA:ED The Lady,* p. 428.
103. This paragraph is not in *Clare of Assisi: Early Documents.*
104. Jacques de Vitry, *Opera omnia* Tubingen–Leipzig 1904, pp. 94–101.
105. H. Grundmann, *Movimenti religosi nel Medioevo,* p. 170.
106. R. Manselli, *La religiosita popolare nel Medioevo,* Rome 1975, p. 12.
107. Jacques de Vitry *Prediche alle beghine,* in *Historiches Jahrbuch* XXXV (1914) p. 46.
108. Cf R. M. Bell *Holy Anorexia,* Chicago–London 1985.
109. This was different from the moment when Francis insisted that Clare accept the title of Abbess. On this see below Chapter VIII.
110. *LegCl* 18.
111. *LegCl* 17.
112. *LegPer* 2; *Fioretti* XVIII.
113. *2 Cel* 129.
114. Celano *Treatise on the miracles,* Ch III, 14.
115. *3Ag* 31.
116. *RegCl* II, 16–17.
117. *CanProc* III, 16.

CHAPTER SIX

118. *Clara claris praeclara* n. 17.
119. *LegCl* 13.
120. M. Mollat, *La notion de la pauvrete au Moyen Age* LII (1966) n. 149, pp. 5–63.
121. Cf *Everini Steinfeldensis Praepositi Ad S Bernardum* in PL 182, coll. 677–678.
122. *RegnBoll* IX, 3.
123. *RegCl* VI, 2, 10–15.
124. *Clara claris praeclara* n. 17.

125. *1Ag* 15–17.

126. *LegCl* 14; cf *CanProc* III, 14, 32; XII, 6.

127. *Clare d'Assise, Ecrits,* 'Sources chretiennes' 325, Paris 1985, p. 79.

128. *The Privilege of Poverty of Innocent III and the Testament of Clare of Assisi.*

129. *The Book of the Dignity and Excellence of the Order of the Seraphic Mother of Poverty, the Lady St Clare of Assisi.*

130. Mariano of Florence, *Libro della degnità et excellentiae del ordine della seraphica madre delle povere donne sancta Chiara da Assisi,* Florence—S Maria degli Angeli 1986, p. 66.

131. W. Malaczek, *Chiara d'Assisi. La questione dell'autenticità del Privilegium paupertatis e del Testamento,* Milan 1996, p. 68.

132. *TestCl* 42–43.

133. Cf Nikolaus Kuster, *Il Privilegio della povertà e il Testamento di Chiara: autentici o raffinate falsificazione?* in *Forma Sororum* 37, (2000) p. 186.

134. Cfr *Caesarii Heisterbacensis Monachi Ord. Cist. Dialogus miraculorum,* I–II, Cologne, Bonn & Bruxelles 1851; I, pp. 77–78.

135. *RegInn* 11.

136. *LegCl* 40.

137. Cf *CA:ED,* p. 86.

138. *CanProc* III, 32.

139. *Clara claris praeclara* n, 1.

CHAPTER SEVEN

140. J–F Godet *Chiara e la vita al femminile* in *Chiara: Francescanesimo al femminile* p. 151.

141. S. Brufani, *Le 'legendae' agiografiche di Chiara d'Assisi,* cit., p. 355.

142. *RegnBull.* XII, 1 & 2.

143. *RegnBull* XII, 4.

144. *RegCl,* I 3–4.

145. *RegCl* VI 1.

146. J. Delarun, *Francesco: un passagio* cit. p. 23.

147. *Ibid,* p. 141.

148. G. Miccoli, *Postfazione* in J. Delarun, *Francesco, un passaggio* cit. p. 184.

149. LegMaj XIII, 1–2.

150. *CanProc* III, 29.

151. *CanProc* IV, 16.

152. E. Pasztor: *Chiara da Montefalco nella religiosita femminile del suo tempo*, in *Santa Chiara da Montefalco e il suo tempo*, Perugia–Florence 1985, p. 203.

153. In the Testament of Clare it says that Francis was 'their pillar, their support and their one consolation after God'. The strong words indicate a debate with the ecclesiastical authorities and implicitly accuse them of not supporting the young community. This is not unlike Francis' own words in his Testament when he said that after 'the Lord gave him brothers, nobody showed me what I should do'. Without re–opening the question of the authenticity of the Testament, if this expression had been invented, it had certainly been well invented as events were to prove in the years following the death of Francis.

154. *CanProc* III, 29.

155. *RegCl* 1, 3.

156. *Dicta B. Aegidii Ord. Minorum*, n. 73 in *Acta Sanctorum*, April XXIII, t.III, Paris 1866, 238b–239a.

157. 2 Cel 13.

158. 2 Cel 207.

CHAPTER EIGHT

159. M. P. Alberzoni, *Papato e nuovi ordini* p. 227.

160. BF I, III, p. 3 cf *CA:ED*, pp. 336–337.

161. *CA:ED*, p. 110.

162. M. P. Alberzoni, *Papati e nuovi ordini* cit. p. 238.

163. *CA:ED*, p. 129.

164. *CA:ED*, p. 130.

165. *LegCl* 27.

166. *BFI* p. 36, *CA:ED*, p. 345.

167. This letter, dated early in 1228, and written before the canonisation of Francis on 16 July, is only to be found in Wadding, *Annales Minorum* ad ann. 1251. CF also *BF* I, p. 37, n. 17.

168. *LegCl* 14.

169. AFH 5 (1912), pp. 445–446.

170. *CA:ED*, p. 87.

171. BF I, p. 143, *CA:ED*, p. 353.

172. BF I, p. 236; *CA:ED*, p. 356.
173. *Angelis gaudium* BF I, p. 242: *CA:ED*, p. 360.
174. Cf *Cum harum rector* of Innocent IV, BF II, p. 184.
175. See above, Chapter One.
176. 8 August 1247, BF I, pp. 476–483: *CA:ED* p. 90 where the text is slightly different.
177. *Ibid.*
178. *ConstHug* 4.
179. *RegCl* II, 12.
180. *ConstHug* 6.
181. *RegCl* V, 3.
182. BF *Epitome*, pp. 284–286.
183. *RegCl* 1, 2.
184. *De Conditoris omnium* BF I, p. 241.
185. *Ibid.*
186. M.P. Alberzoni, *Nequaquam a Christi sequela. Chiara d'Assisi e la memoria di Francesco. Fara Sabina, 18–20 maggio 1994,* Fara Sabina–Rieti 1995, pp. 41–65.

CHAPTER NINE

187. Bertran de Born, *Bem platz le gais temps de pascori,* in *La Poesia dell'eta cortese,* ed. A. Roncaglia, Milan 1961.
188. F. Cardini, *Francesco d'Assisi,* Milan 1989, p. 42.
189. J. Le Goff, *La civiltà dell'Occidente medievale,* Florence 1969, p. 95.
190. Quoted in L. Poliakov, *Storia dell'antisemitismo,* vol. I, Florence 1971, p. 52.
191. *Leviticus* 13.45–46.
192. Quoted in J. Le Goff cit., p. 374.
193. *Testament* 1 and 27.
194. *3 Companions* 58.
195. 1 Cel 23.
196. 2 Cel 37.
197. 2 Cel 108; *LegPer* 81.
198. *LegPer 110.*
199. *CanProc* I, 1.

200. *LegCl* 24–26.
201. *CanProc* VI, 6.
202. *LegPer* 44.
203. *LegCl* 2.
204. *LegCl* 21, cf also *CanProc* II, 20; III, 18; IV, 14; IX, 2; X, 9; XII, 8; XVIII, 6.
205. *CanProc* IX, 2.
206. *CanProc* III, 18.

Brand
Frozen

MARCO BARTOLI is professor of medieval history at the University of Perugia and has done extensive studies on the life of Clare of Assisi.

SISTER FRANCES TERESA DOWNING, O.S.C., is guardian of a community of four Poor Clares in Hastings (Sussex), England. From Cambridge University she earned a diploma in philosophy of religion and theology, religious history and ethics. She is completing a master's degree in philosophy of Franciscan theology and spirituality from the Franciscan International Study Centre at Canterbury, where she teaches about Clare. She wrote *Living the Incarnation: Praying with Francis and Clare of Assisi* and *This Living Mirror: Clare of Assisi*, in addition to editing *Praying in the Franciscan Spirit* and translating five books by Italian authors.